Formerly Special Professor of Management, David Drennan is Chairman and Founder of Good People Management Ltd., the international consultancy company.

His clients include: British Telecom, Coca-Cola, the Bank of England, General Motors, British Aerospace, Castrol, Her Majesty's Treasury, Siemens, Volvo and many others.

His books include: *Transforming Company Culture*, *12 Ladders to World Class Performance* and *Winning the Executive Job Race*.

D1512859

David Drennan

Dedication

I devote this book to my late wife Dee, whose unstinting love and support over the years has been such a jewel in my life.

David Drennan

THE MAGIC OF THE OK BOX

AUSTIN MACAULEY PUBLISHERS™

LONDON • CAMBRIDGE • NEW YORK • SHARJAH

Copyright © David Drennan (2018)

The right of David Drennan to be identified as author of this work has been asserted by him in accordance with section 77 and 78 of the Copyright, Designs and Patents Act 1988.

All rights reserved. No part of this publication may be reproduced, stored in a retrieval system, or transmitted in any form or by any means, electronic, mechanical, photocopying, recording or otherwise, without the prior permission of the publishers.

Any person who commits any unauthorised act in relation to this publication may be liable to criminal prosecution and civil claims for damages.

A CIP catalogue record for this title is available from the British Library.

ISBN 9781788781336 (Paperback)
ISBN 9781788781343 (Hardback)
ISBN 9781788781350 (E-Book)

www.austinmacauley.com

First Published (2018)
Austin Macauley Publishers Ltd™
25 Canada Square
Canary Wharf
London
E14 5LQ

Acknowledgements

Grateful acknowledgement is made to the publishers who have granted permission to use the following material: From *Work and the Nature of Man*, by Frederick Herzberg, copyright 1966, published by Staples Press, and used with permission. From *Profit Sharing and Profitability*, by D Wallace Bell and Charles G Hanson, first published in 1987, by Kogan Page, and used with permission. David Drennan wishes to thank all the companies with whom he has worked over the years, and from whom he learned so much.

Introduction

This is the story of how a young manager, Philip Walker, gets the opportunity to learn early in his career about three powerful but little understood principles that make the difference between being an ordinary people manager and becoming a great people manager. Luckily, he has the chance to spend time at Highfield House – also known as People Management University – in one-to-one conversations with the Professor.

The Professor is well aware that many managers find dealing with people the hardest part of their job. He has seen companies introduce many changes to handle the problem, he has seen many people management fads and techniques come and go. But managing people means you are dealing with human nature, and the laws of human nature do not change. Working <u>with</u> human nature makes people management easy, but otherwise managing people will always be a struggle.

Over the years the Professor has examined many options, and through the trials and tribulations, the bruises and the battles, three fundamental principles stand out above all the rest. These are super important. Interestingly, they are not all that complicated, but these are what really make the difference. These are what every aspiring people manager needs to know – and practise!

Philip Walker's company thinks he is already a manager with good future potential, but they know that as any manager rises in the ranks, they manage increasingly larger numbers of people, and being able to do that well is a factor critical to their future success. That's why they are sending him to People Management University early; they don't just want him to be a good people manager, they want him to be a great people manager.

For his part, Philip is pleased to go. Anything that makes people management easier, he wants to know. He finds the avuncular professor to be a great storyteller, and the principles he explains make such great sense. But Philip has never heard them expressed that way before. They seem so clear, so simple.

And when he hears other enthusiastic managers tell stories of the magic they work in their widely different companies, he soon becomes an enthusiast himself. He can't wait to get started. He can see these really are principles he is going to be using for the rest of his life.

Chapter 1

Philip is gazing out of the window in his office, lost in thought. He was appointed to his first management position just over a year ago, and generally things have been going pretty well. He feels he has made some definite improvements in the running of his department over that time, but it hasn't all been plain sailing. For example, his latest idea met with some opposition from another department just that morning, and as he is wondering what he can do about it, there's a knock at his door. It's the Operations Director's secretary.

"The Operations Director would like to see you in his office on Friday at 2 o'clock," she says.

"The Operations Director? Did he say what it's about?" he asks.

"When I asked him if I could tell you what the meeting was about, he said it was 'personal'."

"Well, thanks for the message. I'll be there," said Philip. 'Personal? What does that mean?' he wondered. Just that morning, he had been reading in the newspaper about two banks shedding thousands of staff to 'stay competitive'. 'And the meeting is on Friday afternoon,' he thought... 'it's not some kind of layoff, is it?' His mind started racing.

That night, he confided in his wife, Julia, that he was a bit worried. "I don't think it can be anything serious," she said consolingly. "Anyway, I thought you were doing well."

"I think I have been," said Philip, "but 2 o'clock on a Friday afternoon...it's a bit worrying. A lot of companies have been cutting back recently, and when managers get given the bad news, Friday afternoon is usually when they get told." Fortunately, just at that point, Philip's three-year-old son was climbing on his knee, fretting for his attention, and that soon took his mind off the subject. But later, he found himself looking at his son as he played and thinking his father might soon be out of a job.

In the following days, Philip seemed to be working harder than ever, almost as if to prove he was a manager worth keeping. By chance, he bumped into the Operations Director in the corridor and gave him a hopeful smile. But his deadpan expression did not give Philip any comfort. 'Should he steel himself for the worst,' he wondered?

Finally the fateful hour arrived, and Philip made his way to the Director's office.

He sat down rather gingerly. "As you know, Philip," the Director began, "companies these days have no alternative but to stay slim and efficient if they want to succeed, and we know that a big part of staying competitive is the quality of people we've got..." Philip gulped. "Fortunately, I'm pleased to tell you that you're one of the people we think has good development potential in this business, and we're happy to have you." Internally, Philip heaved a great sigh of relief as he felt the tension drain away. 'Phew! Thank goodness for that!'

"We're well aware of the value of developing our own good talent," the Director went on. "That's why, we want you to go to Highfield House." It sounded special.

"Highfield House?" queried Philip. "Yes, I'll tell you about it," said the Director.

So saying, he rose from his chair and moved to a whiteboard in his room. "One of the hardest things in management, but one of the most important, is the ability to manage people well. And as you rise in the management ranks, this is what happens." At this point, he drew two triangles on the board, and named them 'work' and 'people', till the drawing looked like this.

12

"Most people are employed to do hands-on work," he continued, drawing line 1, "and although they may deal with other people in the course of a day, most of their time is spent getting the hands-on work done.

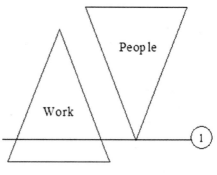

"As they become managers (he then draws line 2), they find they are doing less of the hands-on work and spending much more of their time managing, motivating and organising their people. And at senior

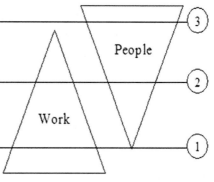

management level (he draws line 3), pretty well all the work you get done is through other people. You may be the best technical person in the business, Philip, but if you can't manage other people, your chances of succeeding in senior management are very small.

"Now we think you have the potential to get there, but people management skills are going to be critically important to your progress. Managers are often just left to follow their own instincts in this respect, but not here. We know there are some fundamental skills that need to be learnt, skills that you will find yourself using for the rest of your life. That's why we want you to go to Highfield House. If anyone knows about good people management, it's the people at Highfield."

"Sounds good to me," enthuses Philip, "but what happens there?"

"Well, you'll meet the Professor for a start. All first-timers have at least one session with the Professor. He's a fascinating character. He's full of stories, and the principles he describes seem so simple, but make no mistake, they're the kind of principles that apply in so many situations, you'll wonder how you ever managed before without knowing them!

"Then you'll have the chance to mix with other managers from all sorts of different companies and hear how they actually use the principles in practice. That will really open your eyes. You'll find that many of the managers there go back every few years for a 'top-up' to learn a bit more and share their own experiences with other people. That's one of the rules at Highfield, by the way. You have to be prepared to share your ideas and experience with others, that's part of the deal.

"Now, sending people to Highfield is not cheap, Philip. We don't send everybody there. We need to be sure that the people we do send are prepared to get the best out of it. Do you think you're ready for that?"

"Absolutely!" says Philip. "I'm just glad to have the opportunity."

When he emerges from the Director's office, Philip is on a high. He can't stop smiling. Once back in his office, he closes the door and immediately gets on the phone to his wife. When he hears that familiar voice on the end, he says: "Darling...remember I was a bit worried about that meeting with the Operations Director. Well, it wasn't about getting fired at all. Apparently, I'm one of their managers with 'potential'," he said grandly, "and I'm to go to Highfield House...I must tell you about it when I get home. It sounds quite a place. I'm really looking forward to it now."

"Sounds like a vote of confidence, Philip," said Julia, delighted.

"Yes, I think it does," said Philip. Finally, he put the phone down and sat back…'Maybe Fridays are not so bad after all,' he thought.

In the next few weeks, Philip is expecting a bundle of reading material to arrive as pre-work before his course, but none arrives. In the week before he is due to go, he decides to phone up Highfield to say he hasn't received any pre-work yet. The lady on the end of the telephone says: "No. No pre-work is required. All you have to do is bring yourself, and be ready to learn. The learning experience is all here." Goodness, thinks Philip, even the reception staff know the answers to these questions straight off. It's not like the usual University. It must be quite a place.

When the day finally arrives, Highfield House turns out to be a large, stone, turreted building set in rolling countryside. As Philip guides his car gently along the driveway through the beautiful wooded grounds up to the house, he says to himself, 'I think I'm going to like it here'. He soon finds himself in the coffee bar with a group of other participants. They seem a friendly, outgoing bunch.

"Have you been here before, Philip?" asks one.

"No," says Philip, "have you?"

"Oh yes, you'll find many of us have. You never stop learning, as you know, and this is one of the best places to get a recharge and take your learning a bit further. But if this is your first time, you won't have met the Professor yet. You'll be having some one-on-ones with him. You'll find that quite a stimulating experience."

"He sounds a bit daunting, a bit frightening," volunteers Philip.

"No, he's not like that at all. He's very approachable, very practical. You'll find he asks you a few searching questions, mind you, and he certainly makes you think. But there's nothing wrong with that, is there?"

"Well, I suppose not," says Philip rather hesitatingly.

Meeting the Professor

Philip has an appointment to meet the Professor next day, and when they finally meet, he finds a tall man of some years with white hair, but he senses a youthful energy and self-assurance that belies his years.

"Have you had a chance to look around the place, Philip? How do you like it?" the Professor asks.

"I think it's a beautiful setting here," responds Philip. "I love the quietness and all the greenery, it's very tranquil. I didn't realise you have this great lake here and the woods behind. I had a walk around yesterday when I arrived, and it's a real picture when you see the deer up by the woods and the swans gliding along the water. It would be a pleasure to come here anytime."

"You know, I sometimes sit here on an evening with the window open, with the sun going down over the lake. We've got a blackbird who's made his home in that tree there, and every evening, about the same time, you hear him singing his heart out. I just sit quietly and listen. He makes the whole scene beautiful."

Soon they turn to business, and the Professor asks Philip if he has been on management training courses before. When Philip says he has, the Professor asks him what the courses actually were, and how he has used the material and the learning since. Philip struggles a bit to remember all the subjects involved, but he does remember getting lots of paperwork each time. And sheepishly, he has to confess that for the most part, it has generally lain untouched in his office cupboard ever since.

"That's not the way we work here," the Professor says. "Of course, we use written materials, videos and a lot of interactive techniques, but we believe that it's the simple fundamental principles – **those you can remember and carry around in your head** – which actually influence your daily management behaviour and will make a real measurable difference to your future managerial habits. When you leave here, you won't have a great manual, which you then leave to gather dust in your desk drawer. But we don't expect you ever to manage in quite the same way again."

The Professor explained that on this, his first visit to Highfield, Philip and he would have three separate sessions together. In each, he would explain a single principle in some detail, after which Philip would spend time with other practising managers at Highfield who have come on return visits, and who would show Philip just how they use that principle in practice. These discussions would not only reinforce his learning, he would learn about the practical problems of implementation and the great variety of ways in which the principles can be successfully applied.

"Let's start then, Philip."

The OK Box

"If you are ever going to manage people effectively, Philip," he begins firmly, "the individuals in your team need to be crystal clear about just what is required of them to do a good job, about the standards they need to achieve, about what is OK and what is not OK."

At this point, the Professor draws a solid square on a whiteboard on the wall and says, "I call it the OK Box".

He explains that the first OK Box we ever encounter in life happens when mother decides it is no longer acceptable for baby to continue using a nappy. She decides Young Johnny should now be capable of controlling his bodily functions and ought to do what is required in his potty.

"Basically," the Professor continues, "mother is saying: in the pot is OK, outside is not OK; and she starts to teach her young son this new lesson. At first, baby doesn't know what sitting on the potty is for, and simply plays around.

Mother waits patiently, but frustratingly at first, nothing much happens.

"But now, when Johnny continues to do things in his nappy, his mother makes grizzly noises, calls him 'naughty' and treats him more roughly. He soon gets the message that there is something which seems to be 'not OK'. What mother is doing, of course, in a perfectly natural way, is encouraging the behaviour she <u>does</u> want to see and discouraging the behaviour she <u>does not</u> want to see.

"When Johnny finally does use the potty, mother looks delighted, praises him loudly and makes a great fuss. "Good boy!" she says, "Well done!" Now at this point in his development, mother is probably the biggest character in Johnny's life: she is the source of his protection, food, warmth and affection.

"So, in the child's mind, staying inside the OK Box becomes strongly associated with (the Professor adds each word to the board as he talks) acceptance . . . affection . . . love . . . and just as important . . . security. Outside the OK Box, on the other hand, becomes associated with trouble . . . suffering . . . pain . . . and what Freud

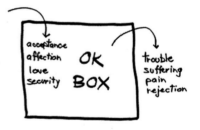

said was the worst punishment . . . rejection.

"Now, because these experiences happen so early in the child's life, it has a deep and enduring psychological effect. We all have a natural tendency to please the person in authority in our lives, because from our earliest days we have strong *emotional* associations that doing so makes for a much more pleasant existence, and no one wants trouble and suffering if they can avoid it. And that's basically where our conscience comes from, from our parents teaching us right from wrong, what is OK and what is not OK."

"That's fascinating," Philip commented. "It all seems so obvious when you say it."

"Well," the Professor continued, "at work you are *in loco parentis*. Where parents are the persons in authority in the home, managers are in the same position at work. And the people you manage would much prefer to stay in your good books, to do a good job for you. What's your experience, Philip? Do you think people prefer to do a good job or to do just as much as they can get away with?"

"I think they much prefer to do a good job," Philip quickly responded.

"I agree, but they need to know what that 'good job' looks like. You see, consciously or sometimes unconsciously, managers effectively decide in their mind what kind of performance or behaviour they are willing to settle for. That becomes their unspoken OK Box. And because the Box has these strong positive and negative associations so early in our lives, it has a very powerful effect on our behaviour.

"People like to know when they are doing the right thing, to feel comfortable that they are in line with the person in authority. That is why, when the manager is clear and sets high expectations, his people tend to respond with above average results and productivity. But if he is vague or inconsistent, he will get no more than patchy, mediocre performance at best."

"So, what you are saying is: if **I** am not clear about that in the first place, I'm not going to get the performance I'm hoping for," Philip suggested.

"Don't just hope, Philip," said the Professor, "be clear. People love to do a good job, but, please, what is that good job? Don't leave people to guess, spell it out and the vast majority of the time, people will do just that. But if you're inconsistent, they'll be inconsistent too, and performance will gradually deteriorate."

"When you say 'inconsistent', what do you mean exactly?"

"Let me give you a simple example," says the Professor, drawing another OK Box on his whiteboard. "Let's assume everyone is due to start work at 9 o'clock in the morning. George, one of the staff, wanders in at 9.08 and simply sits

down at his desk to start work. That's not inside the Box, it's outside (he draws a cross outside the Box). The manager notices but feels a bit reluctant to complain about it. After all, it's only a few minutes. But the Box is not its original size any more, it's this size now (he draws a dotted line round the cross). A few days later, George appears at 9.12. The manager looks skyward and sighs but decides not to get too heavy about

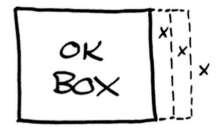

it. But now the Box is this size (he draws another dotted line).

"When finally George turns in one morning at 9.20 (he draws another cross further out), the manager storms over and gives George a loud dressing-down in the hearing of all his colleagues. The manager feels righteous, but George is resentful. The office is disturbed. Some of George's colleagues think it's time he was told a thing or two, but others feel sympathetic at the way he's been treated. A frost descends on the work area. Not the way to run an effective team.

"You see, Philip, silence is acceptance. I'm going to repeat that…" So saying, he draws a big box on his whiteboard and emphasises each word as he writes it in the box: SILENCE…IS… ACCEPTANCE.

SILENCE
IS
ACCEPTANCE

"If the manager says nothing when they act outside the Box, everyone assumes it's OK to be a bit late. The actual behaviour you get is not what you asked for, what you hoped for or even pray for: it is what you accept. Your real OK Box is not shown by what you say, but by what you accept in practice every day".

"Actions speak louder than words, I suppose," Philip offers.

"Absolutely!" the Professor confirms. "High standards of performance don't happen by accident, they start first in the manager's mind. And if they are communicated clearly, realistically and consistently to your people, that is what, with your help and support, they will deliver for you.

"So what about your own people, Philip? Do you think they are all clear about just what is required in the job, about the standards they need to achieve and about how they can measure their own success?"

"Oh, I think they all know what they are doing in my area," Philip hastily replies. "They've been doing it long enough."

"Well, let's take one or two of the jobs as an example and list the requirements, the standards and how they would measure their success," suggests the Professor. Philip does this fairly confidently to start with, but as he is composing the lists, he realises there are some gaps in his knowledge. However, since the Professor does not actually know the jobs, he feels he can bluff it out where he needs to.

"So, if I went to these job holders now, Philip, they would say exactly the same as you, would they?"

"Well, I think they would," Philip replies guardedly.

"You *think* they would. You wouldn't like to take a bet on it, would you?"

Philip was feeling a bit uncomfortable now: "I wouldn't go as far as betting on it," he said.

"Let me help you then," says the Professor. Philip gives a mental sigh of relief.

"Do you have some people who do the same job?"

"Oh yes."

"Do they all do the job the same way?"

"No, they all have their own way of doing things."

The Professor follows up: "Is there one person who does the job best and most consistently?"

"Yes, they would probably say Paul is the best performer," Philip replies.

"Have you captured exactly what Paul does and made his methods available to everybody else?"

"Err... not really," Philip responds weakly.

"Why not?" asks the Professor. "People love to do a good job, Philip, but remember they need to know exactly what that 'good job' looks like. That's the very first job of the manager – making clear what is required in the job, the standards that need to be achieved and giving staff measures by which they themselves will know when they are doing the job successfully...even when you're not there. That's what we call BOPs."

"BOPs?" Philip queries.

"Yes, it stands for Best Operating Practice. We encourage managers to capture the methods used by their best performers in any job and to write it down – what they do, how they do it, how they deal with the most common faults, etc., and that becomes the BOP, *the best way we know of doing the job*.

"We can then carefully teach that process to everyone else. That becomes the OK Box for everyone. Fortunately, because people much prefer to do a good job, and provided they have the right equipment and the right training, they can't resist doing it the best way once they know exactly how."

"So, the OK Box is not just about behaviour then, about coming to work on time and so on," says Philip, "it's about performance on the job."

"Of course," says the Professor. "The main reason companies employ people is to fulfil a particular function, to do that job well and, thereby, to make a positive contribution to the performance of the company as a whole. That's why it's important to spell out in everyone's case exactly what a good job looks like. Now that might include being specific on the productivity expected, quality standards, meeting customer requirements, acting as a good team member and so on.

"And there's a great deal of satisfaction in knowing that you're doing a good job. You can take a pride in that. It's good for your self-esteem. And people who feel good about themselves tend to do an even better job. That's why making clear what the OK Box is, is one of a manager's most important tasks.

"But rather than listen to any more from me, Philip, I suggest you go and talk to some of our visiting managers about just how they use the OK Box principle in practice. We've got one or two people lined up for you. Jim Nixon is your first. You are due to meet him at 2 o'clock in Meeting Room 3. I think you'll find it very interesting. All right?" said the Prof., "I'll see you again tomorrow."

As Philip stepped out into the fresh air and along the gravel path to the main building, his thoughts wandered as he walked along. 'I can see now why you don't need a great treatise to understand the OK Box principle,' he thought. 'It's immediately obvious what it means, it's easy to remember, and you can apply it to so many different things.

'And although I hate to admit it, the Professor was quite right when he challenged me about whether I had really spelled out the job in detail for everybody. I suppose that's why they're forever asking me if this is all right, or that's all right...and it all takes up a lot of time. Maybe that's also why I get pretty variable performances from time to time. It will be interesting to see how the other managers handle that...'

The OK Box in Practice

Philip arrived a minute before time at the door of Meeting Room 3 and could see someone already there beckoning him in. Jim Nixon turned out to be a man in his late thirties with a ready smile. He greeted Philip warmly as if welcoming him as a new member into the club. "How did it go with the Prof? Did you find yourself struggling for answers some of the time?"

"Only when he asked me to make a list of the requirements of two or three of my people's jobs and their standards of performance," said Philip. "I realised I had to fill in a few gaps off the top of my head, but I thought since he didn't know the jobs, I could bluff my way through. Then he asked me if I would bet that the job holders would all say the same as I had written down. Well, since nothing is written down in some cases, I realised he had got me there."

"Well, if that's all, there's nothing to worry about," said Jim encouragingly. "You see, the Prof.'s got this view that if the principle is not simple enough for you to carry around in your head, it won't affect your everyday behaviour. And it has to, I think, if it's going to be of any benefit to you. And although the OK Box is a simple principle, it's profound. You find yourself using it in so many different places."

"So how do you use it in your company?" asks Philip.

"I work for an electronics company," Jim explains. "We make coin mechanisms for vending machines, gaming machines, coin counting equipment and so on. There's a lot of manual assembly work involved, wiring, soldering, attaching screws, etc.

"It's not easy maintaining high productivity and good quality at the same time in these situations. Some companies pay output bonuses, but we know when you do this, quality inevitably suffers as people try to push through not quite OK products to make their bonus numbers. We couldn't do that

– working for our customers, our quality standard had to be zero defects!

"So, this is what we did. We told all our people that quality comes first. When we sell our product to our customers, we effectively promise them that it will do exactly what we say it will do...not some of the time, but all of the time. That is our first priority.

"So, we said: 'Don't ever pass on any product to the next person in the line unless it allows them to do a zero-defect job. And when they take the part from you, we want that next person to check the part is perfect before they do any further work on it. The product is never going to be right for the customer unless it is right at every stage of manufacture.

"We want our quality to be so good, our customers don't ever want to go anywhere else. And we will do whatever it takes to ensure we can do the job right first time – that is not only our cheapest way to manufacture, it also makes the most reliable product for the customer. So, make no mistake," said Jim, in an insistent tone, "QUALITY COMES FIRST."

"Goodness," said Philip, "that's pretty clear."

"That's an OK Box we just can't compromise on," Jim continued. "When we start with a new product, we go as slow as we need to, to make sure we get the quality right first time. However, if we don't make good quality cheap enough, then we can't match the competition on price, and we don't get the business. And if we don't make a profit in addition, we don't get to stay in business. So, that's where productivity becomes very important."

"But how did you get good productivity without compromising your product quality?" Philip queried.

"I'll show you. My boss is a great believer in using the power of **expectations**, and I have to say, so am I. First of all – and this is important – we make sure our people have everything they need to do a good job: the right materials, the right equipment, the right training. No point in expecting them to do a good job if they haven't got that. Then, in discussion with our people actually doing the job, we work out what should be the <u>expected</u> productivity per hour. That then becomes the 'expected' line on our productivity graph."

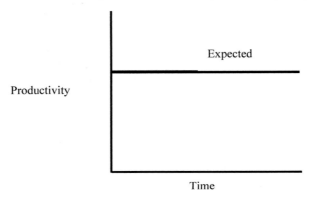

At this point, Jim goes over to the whiteboard, draws the 'X' and 'Y' axes of a graph and then a heavy line across the graph which he names 'expected'. "We make clear to everyone that not achieving that standard would be a real failure. It's just like the OK Box: meeting or even beating the expected line is OK, but not making the line is definitely not OK."

"So you actually draw an expected line on the graph from the very start?" asked Philip.

"Yep. That's the level of performance we know can be achieved, so we normally make it stand out, and we post the performance graphs right next to where people operate so they can see them every day. That way, no one has any doubt about what's required."

"And do you find people generally meet the expected productivity line?" asked Philip.

"Oh, yes," said Jim. "Mind you, we only set targets which are realistic, that's important, and remember we agree these with the people actually doing the job. Fundamentally, we treat people like adults, but we also expect them to act like adults – in other words, to meet their targets and do the job well <u>without supervision</u>. We trust them to do the right thing and get on with the job whether we are there or not –

that's what we expect. And by and large, I'm happy to say that's just what they do. But I might have an actual graph with me that I can show you."

So saying, he dug into his briefcase to see what he could find…"Yes, here we are…coin flight decks…flight decks are the channel where coins inserted in the machine fall down a slot and are checked for shape, weight, thickness and so on," said Jim as he laid the graph out on the table.

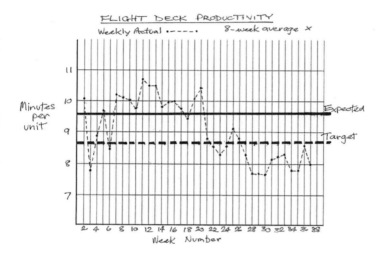

"The measure is minutes taken per unit – that's the figure down the left hand side – so if we are doing well, this is a graph where we would expect to see a falling line. We plot our performance each week so we can see if we're trending in the right direction. Obviously, we've done quite well here." They seem to have started off all right, Jim, and then they appear to have lost it for a few weeks, about week 12. What happened there?" Philip asked.

"Yes, you're quite right, Philip. Well spotted." Jim chided. "We had several problems with our equipment there – between weeks 10 and 20 – where the results went the wrong way, and we had a new person on the line at the same time, so it took us a little while to get everything back on track.

"But each team meets first thing every morning with their Team Leader and goes through yesterday's performance, the problems they encountered, what they can do about them and so on. They never forget just what the OK Box is."

"You have another line on the chart, Jim...this dotted 'target' line. What's the significance of that?"

"Well," Jim answered, "the expected line is quite a demanding achievement, but we know we'll get a bit complacent and stale if we don't challenge ourselves a bit, if we don't keep trying to improve."

"So, once we see ourselves hitting the expected line with some regularity and confidence, we get the team together and ask: 'What do you think we could go for now, guys?' That often leads to discussion about what would make the job easier, better or faster and sometimes we get up a bit of bravado...you know, like: 'we don't quite know how we are going to do it, but let's go for it anyway.' And it's amazing how creative and motivated teams can get when they get the bit between their teeth. And, as you can see, they've done really well on the flight deck."

"So the OK Box is not just something imposed by management," Philip ventured.

"Not at all," retorted Jim. "As I was saying earlier, we treat people like adults. We tell them the facts. They know that our business will be no better than we can make it together. All our livelihoods and job security are tied up in doing right for the customer, in doing it better than the competition, and doing it cost-effectively. The OK Box is what we need to do and what we know we're capable of. We're serious about it, people understand that and we all work at it together."

Just then two faces appeared at the door: "Is it OK to come in?"

"Sure," said Jim, "come and meet Philip here. Philip, this is Marion George; she works for one of the big banks here."

Marion was a slim young lady with a friendly face beneath her dark, wavy hair. "Nice to meet you, Philip. How are you doing?" she asked brightly.

"Well, I'm certainly learning things," said Philip.

"You will, you will," said a booming voice next to Marion. "Hello, Philip, I'm Cobus McKenzie, how do you do?" Cobus was a well-built, black man well over six feet tall with a huge smile that lit up his face and spread from ear to ear.

Jim chipped in again: "Philip, I obviously come from a manufacturing environment, but we thought it would be good for you to hear how people implement the OK Box in service companies as well. Cobus, tell Philip about your company in South Africa."

"I work for a company that runs game lodges, Philip."

"Game lodges!" said Philip, immediately interested.

"We're run by a boss, Dave Barton, who started off taking foreign visitors into the bush to see lions, elephants, giraffes, crocodiles and all the other wild life. Dave realised that Africa has this huge asset, which can not only thrill visitors from around the world, but create employment and help conservation at the same time. So he founded our present company, Africa Inc., and established our company mission of: 'Care of the animals, care of the people, care of the environment'. He's really passionate about it, he's a real inspiration to us.

"But although visitors expect a few bumps in their Land Rovers as you look for animals in the bush, they also expect the hotel standards that they have experienced in Europe or the US when they get back to their lodges in the evening. We deliberately employ people from the local villages close to our game lodges, but they haven't experienced hotel standards anywhere. So it's quite a task teaching them how to deliver that kind of high level service, as you can imagine. For example, how do you teach them what a deluxe bathroom should look like when it's prepared, when no one in their village has even got a bathroom!"

"Wow," said Philip, "that's a tough job."

"I should add," Cobus went on, "that the vast majority don't speak English and can't read or write, so that makes it even tougher."

"Goodness," said Philip, "and I thought I had problems! How do you handle that then, Cobus?"

"Well, we use pictures, and we do a lot of showing. Our Team Leaders do speak English, and we have a big BOPs manual, which lays out exactly how it should be in the bedrooms, at front of house, in the reception car park, in the Land Rovers, at evening bush dinners and all the rest. These are the standards that we want to be typical of Africa Inc., our OK Box, if you like.

"So, when we're training our people, we show them exactly what a good job looks like. We have a routine we follow, which goes: **show, tell, do, repeat**. In other words, we **show** them, say, just how the bedroom should look when it has been properly prepared, and we **tell** them why it needs to be like that.

"Then we get them to **do** it by themselves, and we **repeat** it until they can do it by heart. And, you know, they love to do a good job. I suppose they're just like people anywhere else in the world. But I love it when I see their big smiles when they get everything right, and I give them a pat on the back. It really touches my heart."

Philip hadn't expected such emotional sensitivity from a big man like Cobus, but it was quite obvious that he meant it. He thought to himself, 'In the end, people are people round the world. With the OK Box, not only does the company get the right job done, but doing a good job can give people real personal satisfaction.' Philip then probed Cobus a bit further: "But like all service businesses, I suppose things can go wrong from time to time. How do you keep the standards up?"

"We do several things," replied Cobus. "Every week, we hold meetings where we read back the guest comments, good and bad, to our people, and we decide what we have all learnt from that. That's very useful.

"Then, we do little unannounced audits to see how we're keeping our standards up. People who get a perfect audit three times in a row get a special credit which stands them in good stead for promotion. Sometimes, the Team Leader will take a member of staff with them and get them, the staff members, to do the audit. I can tell you, they learn a lot that way.

"We've now got 22 lodges in Africa, and people develop different good ideas, as you can imagine. So we've taken these as we've found them and built them into our BOPs. In quite a few cases, we've got the written standard for, say, bush dinners, the OK Box standard. Then we've got level 2 standard, which is what you can do to please the guests even more and level 3 if you really want to delight them.

"Funnily enough, once staff know what these ideas are, they just can't resist doing them! I guess that's one of the reasons we get cards from what I would call pretty sophisticated guests telling us that their time in Africa was their holiday of a lifetime. That gives us all a very warm feeling."

"So that means, Cobus," said Philip, "that with the OK Box you're training people from pretty poor villages, illiterate or with very little education, to deliver the kind of service that delights even customers used to the very best standards elsewhere in the world. That's amazing."

"Quite frankly, Philip," said Cobus, "I think the OK Box will work anywhere in the world. I'm not saying our people are perfect all the time, they're not. But they definitely know what a good job looks like, and the vast majority of the time that's just what they do. My view is that whether people live in Africa or in Great Britain, whether they have had only a rudimentary education or a high level one, they still like the self-satisfaction of knowing they're doing a good job."

Turning to Marion, Cobus said "Marion, your working environment is quite different from ours. What do you think?"

Marion, who had been listening intently to all of this, immediately agreed, adding: "My mind boggles when I listen to Cobus and hear all the problems he has to deal with. We work in lovely conditions in our bank offices, the people we work with can certainly all read and write – I suppose we don't appreciate how lucky we are. But even with highly educated people doing pretty demanding jobs, we still find having company standards to work to a very important factor in getting consistent good performance.

"For example, we used to get complaints that letters and other communications sent from the bank looked different depending on which department they came from. Often they would have fairly obvious spelling mistakes, or funny punctuation, or even fancy headings and lettering if the secretary concerned liked experimenting with the fonts on her computer and so on.

"Eventually, we got so many comments we started asking ourselves 'should we have a standard we all work to; should we describe what is OK and what is not OK?' After all, every communication we send out makes a statement about us, it forms our image in the eyes of the customer. And wouldn't we want to appear the kind of bank that seems to have got its act together, the kind of bank who took the trouble to get things right? Well, there's lots of things you have to get right to please today's customers, but that's something that doesn't cost anything which we could work on straight away."

"What did you do then?" asked Philip. "Get your senior office manager to lay out the rules?"

"No, we wanted the people themselves to be involved. So, we put together a little project team composed of eight secretaries all from different departments, and asked them to tell us what they thought the standards ought to be," Marion responded. "We find people bristle at standards forcefully imposed from above; somehow they feel treated a bit like children. But when they feel real ownership for the standards, there's much more commitment to making them work in practice."

"And did it work?" asked Philip.

"It took them several weeks, meeting for a day a week, to put it all together. At the end, we had them present their proposals to meetings of departmental heads. That went down very well; they even drew some rounds of applause. So, with a few modifications as a result of feedback from the meetings, that has become our standard, our 'OK Box' for reports and letters.

"People know now what font to use, how big the margins should be, how the headings should look, that there will be no spelling mistakes, etc. And our secretaries feel they are making a positive contribution to the good image we present to our customers. And of course, they're doing just that."

"I like the idea of getting the actual job holders to compose their own standards," said Philip, "composing their own OK Box. It's a bit difficult to say the standards are not practical if they themselves proposed them!"

"Exactly," agreed Marion. "But we find you particularly need standards and an OK Box for things that happen all the time."

"All the time? What do you mean?" said Philip.

"For example, meetings."

"Meetings!" they all exclaimed in chorus. "I hate meetings!" said Jim.

"I know how you feel, Jim," Marion sympathised. "But we have quite a lot of meetings in the bank, as you'll appreciate. And it was a bit frustrating – you know, people would wander in late, forget to bring their papers, talk over the top of each other, take different messages out of the same meeting, fail to deliver on what they agreed, minutes would take ages to appear and on and on. I don't suppose you have these problems."

"You must be joking!" said Jim. "Of course, we do."

"Well, we decided there was so much to-ing and fro-ing, time wasted, misunderstandings and the rest, that we had to do something about it. We had to have some rules that we all bought, into an OK Box for meetings, if you like. And this is what we wrote..." said Marion, dipping into her briefcase and laying a single sheet out on the table.

33

Rules for Meetings

1. The outcome/purpose of any meeting will be stated in advance, i.e. both when the meeting is first requested, and at the start of the meeting itself.
2. The length of the meeting will be stated up-front, i.e. when first requested, and at the start of the meeting itself. Attendees may leave at any time after the stated time for the meeting has expired.
3. We will all come to meetings we have agreed to attend on time, and start promptly.
4. We will all bring to the meeting any relevant or necessary information, and our diaries.
5. During the meeting: one speaker, one meeting at a time.
6. Phones will be switched off for the duration of the meeting.
7. The person who calls the meeting will produce the minutes.
8. The minutes will be Action Minutes, i.e. who is doing what and when.
9. Minutes will be sent out to attendees within 48 hours.
10. Agreements are commitments, i.e. we will all do whatever is necessary to deliver our personal undertakings.

"Marion, can I have a copy of that?" asked Jim enthusiastically. "We could certainly use it."

"Take that one," said Marion.

"I wouldn't mind a copy as well," said Philip. "And me," said Cobus. They all laughed.

"Sounds like it's a bit of a problem around the world!" said Marion.

"But how does it actually work in practice, Marion?" asked Philip, voicing the scepticism of the others.

"Well, our big boss sticks to it faithfully, and his example definitely sends a message round the place. He's made it part of our culture. But we have a bit of fun with it as well."

"Bit of fun? What do you mean?" asked Jim.

"If people turn up late, we all make hooting noises and knock the table. It can be a bit embarrassing. So you find people scooting along the corridor to get there on time. Also, if you come late or don't bring your diary, for example, you have to contribute £1 to our charity box in the middle of the table. And we all make a great fuss. We try not to get too heavy about it, but they certainly know when it's not OK. You certainly feel guilty if you turn up at the next meeting and haven't managed to deliver. You know you'll have to face the music."

"That's interesting," said Jim, "that's a favourite saying of the Prof. How does he put it now...'*Don't minimise the power of guilt to motivate people into doing the right thing!*'"

"Well, he's right there," said Cobus.

"So," said Jim, looking at Philip, "has all that given you an idea of how the OK Box operates in practice?"

"It certainly has. I had no idea that the OK Box could take so many different forms. You see, I had never even heard of the OK Box before, and when the Prof. explained it to me, it sounded so clear and simple...and powerful. I thought: I can use that. But you guys have definitely broadened my perspective on it all."

"One of the things that may not be immediately obvious, though, Philip," added Marion, "is that the OK Box forces you as the manager to be clear about just what is OK and what is not. Most of us tend to assume that people will just naturally do the right thing without being told. For example, that they will turn up at meetings on time, bring the right information with them, etc. etc.

"But often that's not what happens in practice. Even when people know the meeting starts at 2 o'clock, say, they will wander in at quarter past with some excuse that they were on the phone, implying that speaking just at that instant to whomever was on the phone was more important than keeping ten other people waiting. That's not only impolite, it's such a waste of valuable management time. Why should that be OK? And if you say nothing, of course it just goes on."

"Silence is acceptance, I suppose," said Philip, recalling the Professor's words.

"Exactly that," said Marion emphatically. "Management can get pretty complex at times, but if we can't do the simple things right, what hope have we of doing the complicated things? And when it comes to managing my own team, I'm well aware of the value of making clear what a good job looks like. Not only does the OK Box press you into detailing just what is required on the job, I find my people prefer it. They <u>want</u> to know. What do you think, Jim?"

"I agree wholeheartedly," concurred Jim. "And I'm sure you'll agree with this too, Marion. I try to make it <u>easy</u> for my people to do the right thing. There's no point in saying 'this is how the job has to be done' if the materials are not right, for example, or the equipment is on the blink.

"So I find the pressure is on me to get everything right for them, to remove all the obstacles that might prevent them getting into the OK Box and staying there. Of course, everything doesn't always go right, but when they know I'm really trying, they find ways of getting round the problems. It's very much a two-way street. But we know what we all want to achieve."

"I guess you all feel more of a team too," Philip suggested.

"Yes, that's certainly true in the hospitality industry," said Cobus. "There are so many things to go wrong – small things, niggly things – that if you weren't flexible and working as a team, you would never end up with satisfied customers. But you also find that the OK Box moves over time, Philip. It's like the Olympic Games."

"Like the Olympic Games?"

"Yes. The time that earned the gold medal in the 800 metres last time may not be good enough to win next time. Standards keep improving. And it's the same with us. You remember I told you we described Best Operating Practice for all the jobs we do, then later added additional levels as people came up with new ideas. Eventually, we find just by habit that the higher level naturally becomes our <u>everyday</u> OK Box. I look back only a few years to when we didn't have any BOPs, and I realise how far we've actually come in a relatively short time. I have to say I'm a great believer."

Jim chipped in: "Philip, I guess that's as much as you take in one day. Why don't we adjourn to the bar for a drink? I should think you're ready for one."

"Can I just take a couple of minutes to summarise all the things you've been telling me in my notebook, Jim. I'm afraid if I don't capture it now, it will all escape somehow."

"All right," said Jim. "Come over and join us when you're ready."

* * *

Philip sat down and tried to encapsulate in a few words what he had learned during his first day. First he drew the box, then this was his summary:

- To get the behaviour and performance you would like to see, you need to make your OK Box clear.

Once you do, people will have a strong psychological drive to stay within the Box.

- If people stray outside the OK Box, you need to say something at the time. Otherwise, silence is acceptance.
- The OK Box can take many different practical forms, but the principle remains the same. You need to stay clear and consistent about what is OK and what is NOT OK.
- Like the Olympics, the OK Box's standards of performance may change over time, but the standards should always be realistic.
- Involving staff in agreeing the standards increases their ownership and commitment.

Chapter 2

It was a relaxed evening Philip Walker spent with his new-found friends at Highfield at the end of his first day. He felt he had already learned so much in just one day. His mind churned with thoughts and ideas later in bed as he tried to fall asleep.

The following morning, he decided on a walk in the sunshine before his next session with the Professor. As the Professor greeted him, he asked: "How did you find your meeting with the other managers yesterday, Philip?"

"Fascinating!" replied Philip. "When I first heard about the OK Box principle from you yesterday, I thought, 'That's a great idea; I can definitely use that.' But I had no idea it could take so many forms until I heard the managers talk about it. I mean, Jim Nixon works in manufacturing, Marion is much more in an office environment, and if Cobus is anything to go by, this thing is international, you can use it anywhere."

"Exactly," the Professor responded. "That's what makes it so powerful. You don't need to remember all the examples, all you need to remember is the concept, that's what's important. You'll find you get quite creative in how you implement it as you've seen the other managers do in their companies. As some of them may have told you, I am very much in favour of simple concepts you can carry around in your head and put to work every day.

"So, you have learnt one principle now, Philip. Are you ready for the next one?"

"You bet!" said Philip.

The Greatest Management Principle

"Well," the Prof. began, "this one has been called the greatest management principle in the world," said the Professor.

"The greatest management principle in the world?" echoed Philip.

"Yes, what do you think it is?"

"Mmm...I'm not sure," murmured Philip, hoping for some help.

"Well, you're already a manager, Philip, so what do you think? Have a guess."

"Err...Trust," Philip ventured.

"Yes, that's definitely important," the Professor replied. "I know some managers I would trust, but I wouldn't say that makes them all good managers."

"Good communications," Philip offered.

"Again, useful, but not the principle I'm looking for," the Prof. responded.

"Consistency..." Philip followed up. "Teamwork..."

"No, let me tell you. This is the greatest management principle in the world..." So saying, the Professor brought out a large card and placed it prominently on his desk in front of Philip. It said:

> **The behaviour that gets rewarded gets repeated**

"The behaviour that gets rewarded gets repeated..." murmured Philip.

"Yes, let me explain by going back to basics first," the Professor went on.

"The world-renowned psychologist, B. F. Skinner, conducted many experiments researching animal and human behaviour. He found that he could 'shape' animal behaviour by repeatedly rewarding the behaviour he wanted to see i.e. get them to learn patterns of behaviour they would never have achieved simply by accident. One of his researches was with pigeons." So saying, the Professor started drawing a small cage on his whiteboard with a feeding chute and pigeon inside. They both laughed at his efforts.

"If Skinner wanted to have the pigeon turn, say, a double pirouette clockwise, he would first encourage the bird by rewarding any small movement in that direction with a maize bean. In other words, he rewarded the behaviour he wanted to see. This, he named <u>reinforcement</u>. Soon the bird cottoned on that turning in that direction produced tasty food rewards and repeated the behaviour. Skinner then gradually rewarded only bigger turns until the bird was doing a full double pirouette. From start to finish, the time period involved would be under two minutes! No shouting, no ordering, just rewarding.

"Skinner had in fact discovered a fundamental principle of both animal and human behaviour, namely that <u>the behaviour that gets rewarded gets repeated</u>.

"Of course, we mustn't simply assume that people are like animals, but the principle remains the same. For example, when you're teaching new employees what is required in the job (the OK Box), use some positive reinforcement every time you see your employee making positive efforts in the right direction – by saying "good!", "well done", etc. People can't resist doing more of the same when they feel they are winning – and they begin enjoying the job.

"On the other hand, we all tend to drop the tactics that don't work. We might try some new things, but if they don't produce the success we hoped for, we move on to something else – they become what Skinner called <u>extinguished</u>. That has big implications for all managers. If employees are trying to give something a good effort or make suggestions to improve things but it appears no one notices or shows any appreciation, they soon give up doing it. You have to 'stroke' the behaviour you want to see every time you see it. In other words, you have to <u>encourage</u> people into the OK Box."

"You mean, a bit like Skinner," said Philip interjecting, "you have to encourage even the first signs of people moving in the right direction, so that they do more of it?"

"Exactly. You're getting the idea already, Philip," the Professor replied. "Have you ever wondered how the trainers in aquaria shows get these huge whales to jump right out of the water and hit suspended plastic balls with their nose?"

Philip looked blank.

"They do it first," the Prof. continued, "by laying a rope across the bottom of the pool and rewarding the whale with a small food reward each time it passes over. Then gradually they raise the rope by degrees, each time providing a small reward for swimming over the rope. They 'reinforce' the behaviour they want to see. Eventually the rope is raised way over the water, and this huge whale still heaves itself over. You wouldn't believe it if you didn't see it with your own eyes. It is quite spectacular."

"But when it comes to people, you obviously can't use maize beans or fish as a reward, can you? Does that mean you have to use money rewards to get the behaviour you want to see?" Philip queried.

"No, not at all," the Professor responded immediately. "It's a serious mistake to think that money is the only reward. It's simply not true. Did Jim Nixon show you an example of the productivity charts he uses in his electronics company?"

"Yes, he did. On the chart I saw, the team had improved their productivity over a nine-month period by something like 20%, just using their hand skills – it was quite impressive."

"Well, there was no extra money or bonuses for doing that," the Professor continued. "But they find it rewarding to succeed. And Jim gives them plenty of opportunities to get that good feeling of success.

"For example, when he sits down with his group to discuss his 'expected' productivity line on any new product, the line is a combination of what is needed to make the product cost-effective and what he knows the team can achieve. In other words, he sets it a level where he knows the team has a good chance of winning. As he sees them making progress, he gives them a 'thumbs up' or a pat on the back. These are just little rewards, but they keep encouraging the behaviour he wants to see.

"If they run into difficulties, he doesn't criticise them, he listens to what they say the problems are, and if they are good points, he does something about them immediately. That's a reward for most employees – having managers who listen to what they say. And interestingly, Jim gets a reward back – because they know he listens, they give him even more suggestions about how to improve things and resolve problems. With a team of twelve people, Jim then has twelve brains thinking about improvements instead of just one.

"First thing every morning, Jim has a ten-minute meeting with his team to discuss the problems of the day before and the work for that day. Just the act of standing together as a team with a common purpose five days a week – that's more than 200 times a year – creates a real strong team feeling. That's another reward – feeling you belong somewhere, to a good working team.

"Jim also places the performance charts close to the work area so they can be seen by everyone. They know what they want to achieve, and they love to see themselves making visible progress. The team knows that Jim only accepts that they have achieved his 'expected' line when they've beaten that target for five days in a row. When they do, he sticks one of his 'smiley faces' on the chart – of course, it's only a bit of paper, but the feeling of success it gives them is another reward.

"That success feeling makes them ready to accept another challenge, just to repeat the feeling. That's when they agree with their boss a new target, but again he makes sure they don't take on too much – he still wants them to have a good chance of winning. And when they do, they celebrate and have a bit of fun. That might mean doughnuts or cakes all round and free coffee for the day. It's only a modest reward, but it helps both to mark the achievement and to reinforce that great 'we are winners' feeling.

"Can you see how all this builds up, Philip?"

"I certainly can," replied Philip.

"So, let me emphasise this very important point with you…" the Professor went on, producing a large card from a drawer and placing it in front of Philip.

> **To be a great people manager, you need to create good associations with work**

"That's one of the key jobs of a manager: to make work <u>rewarding</u> for your people. And I don't just mean money.

"I meet managers who think their people only come to work for the money. But these same managers find their people can't wait to get out at the end of the day; they only do as much as they have to; they don't contribute ideas, they leave jobs half done when the bell sounds, and they don't want to do a minute's extra work unless they get paid overtime. If that's the kind of attitude you want, Philip, then just rely on money.

"Of course, the money is important. People want to be fairly paid for the work they have to do. But if you want your people to actually <u>enjoy</u> being at work and especially to enjoy working for <u>you</u>, then you'll build in all these other satisfactions that take no more time and are so simple to do, but make so much difference.

"Treat your people like adults, and expect them to act like adults – showing them that kind of respect raises their self-esteem and is a reward in itself. Listen actively to what they say and to the positive ideas they come up with. And when they see you actually take action on the points they raise; they'll give you even more ideas and enjoy doing it.

"Talk to them frequently as a group so that they get this good feeling of belonging to a team, and a successful one at that. Everyone loves to succeed, so give your team plenty of opportunities to do so – by agreeing sensible achievable targets with them, encouraging them with positive comments as they make progress, and boosting their sense of achievement with fun celebrations when they pass important milestones. There's great satisfaction in working for someone like that."

"I think you're right, Professor," said Philip. "I've already decided on a few changes I'm going to make when I get back to work."

"But there're two main dangers you should be aware of in all this," the Professor added.

"Two main dangers...what are they?" asked Philip.

"The first is not doing it!" came back the reply. "Not making the encouraging comment when you see something good, not expressing a bit of appreciation for a special effort, not offering praise when someone has jumped a learning hurdle and so on. It's so easy to forget.

"Some managers have boasted to me that they manage by 'kicking ass'. That immediately tells me they don't reward the behaviour they most want to see; they manage by penalising the behaviour they don't want to see.

"In that kind of atmosphere, employees expend most of their effort avoiding the boss, keeping out of his way. They don't offer new ideas, they don't go the extra mile, they only do as much as they have to, to keep him off their back and avoid shouting matches. I don't want to work in a place like

45

that. And I can tell you: you're never going to be a great people manager if all you do is 'kick ass'.

"As a matter of interest, Philip, what proportion of the time you take communicating with your people is spent 'kicking ass', i.e. issuing orders, complaining about things as opposed to encouraging and rewarding?"

"Oh, I would have to make a guess I think..." said Philip hesitantly, "...fifty-fifty maybe."

"If I asked your people the same question, what would they say?"

There was a silence. "Don't worry, Philip, I'm not going to ask them," the Prof. continued. Philip looked relieved. "But the point I make is a serious one. Give it some thought, and work on getting the proportions right. Of course, don't devalue your own praise by over-repetition to the point where your people feel your praise takes no effort at all.

"But each time you see a real improvement, say something positive about it, don't let it go unrecognised. And over time, your people will achieve the kind of spectacular results that neither you or they ever thought were possible when you first started. That's the real impact of the Greatest Management Principle in the world. It's a powerhouse."

"You said there was another danger, Professor, what was that?" asked Philip.

"Inadvertently rewarding the behaviour you don't want to see!" came the answer.

"What do you mean – inadvertently?" Philip queried.

"Let me give you a simple example. Do you have any children, Philip?" the Professor asked, apparently suddenly changing the subject.

"Yes, two," Philip replied, "one is five and the other three."

"Sometimes children get upset because you refuse them a lollipop or an ice-cream when it is too near to their mealtime. Then they start crying...loudly. You stand firm and say no. They then start screaming, but you hold firm. They get even louder, people start looking, it becomes

46

embarrassing. You then concede, just to get them to keep quiet. Has that ever happened to you?"

"I'm afraid it has," Philip replied, looking rather sheepish.

"You see, despite our best intentions, we may actually be encouraging the very behaviour we don't want to see. And it happens in business too. Let me illustrate the point.

"Some years ago now, workers in some British industries got into the habit of threatening to go on strike if their pay claim was not met. The companies involved would try to negotiate an agreement but in the end would often declare that this was their 'final offer' and that anything more was 'unaffordable'. When the employees then went on strike, further negotiations would take place, and the company would make further concessions simply to get their people back to work.

"Now, all this is understandable, but it has disastrous consequences. First, employees begin to feel that they simply can't believe what management says – they say one thing but do another. That's bad enough. But secondly the employees seem to do better by not cooperating with the company than by cooperating. That's serious. What do you think would happen in the future then?"

"The company is going to get more of the same," said Philip.

"Precisely. Companies found that non-cooperation became a habit with employees when they got back to work, and it became a daily battle for managers to get things done. That was a real problem. So, by all means, encourage and reward the behaviour you do want to see, but never, even under pressure, reward the behaviour you don't want to see.

"Now, Philip, there are all sorts of encouragements that managers can use, but what kind of rewards work best at work do you think?" asked the Professor.

"The first thing people usually think of is money," Philip replied, "and I think money does work. I mean, people will often put in extra effort to earn a bonus, for example."

"They do," the Professor agreed, "and although money is not by any means the only motivator, it can certainly be motivational in the right format. Some of the reasons for this is that because money is an easily measurable commodity, you can usually see the relation between your effort and your reward, and the extra income gives you the freedom to do additional things outside of work. So it can certainly be a motivator when the pay system is structured well, and we're going to talk about that in a moment.

"Always be careful, though, of the negative aspects and unexpected kick-backs you get when money is the only motivator you use."

"Kick-backs?" queried Philip.

"Yes," the Prof. confirmed. "Sometimes paying a bonus to focus on one aspect of the work costs you a penalty on some other important factor. For example, many companies in the clothing or other production businesses operate on a piecework basis – in other words they tell their employees: the more pieces you produce, the greater will be your pay.

"Unfortunately, that can cause operators to rush things and take shortcuts. And because companies fear quality might suffer, they usually employ quality inspectors to make sure bad quality doesn't get out. Employees often then start arguing with the inspectors about what is OK and what isn't OK. They pressure them to let things go, or they try to hide things from the inspector or 'slip things through'.

"As you can imagine, that puts a lot of tension in the workplace with people working against each other. And with individuals trying to maximise their personal earnings, teamwork, very much, gets relegated to second place. Also, although using money as an incentive can boost productivity, you will never get consistent world-class quality with a piecework pay system in place."

"Does that mean, then," asked Philip, "that if you use money just to focus on one particular thing, you can easily create other problems or unexpected reactions?"

"You can. You need to think it all through. For example, one company called us in to help them with their employee suggestions scheme. Several years before, with good intentions and hoping to interest employees in coming up with ideas for improvements in the business, they had announced a company-wide suggestion scheme. Ideas certainly came forward, but they encountered some intractable problems.

"Only 25% of employees ever put a suggestion forward; 75% never bothered. Arguments developed about how much any suggestion was worth, employees complained about delays in evaluating their ideas or got resentful if their idea was rejected. Some anticipated savings were never realised in practice, and the administrative burden of operating the scheme was heavy.

"But the unspoken message the company had sent to everyone was: 'making suggestions for improvement is not part of your normal job, we pay extra for that.' That view was confirmed when an employee was heard to tell a colleague: 'Don't tell management anything unless they pay you extra for it.' Now, that was a real problem."

"But how can you persuade employees to give you suggestions willingly then, without using money?" Philip asked.

"Good question," the Professor replied. "Make it part of their everyday job. Don't use money as a substitute for good management. Toyota learned that lesson a long time ago."

"Toyota?" Philip queried, hoping to hear more.

"Toyota is one of the biggest car companies in the world, but their employees achieve a consistency of product quality which is unsurpassed. And that's no accident," the Professor went on.

"Several decades ago, the company decided to ask employees to make suggestions for improvement. The first year, the company got about 5,000 suggestions from around 8,000 employees. If you work that out, it's less than one suggestion per person in a whole year. Not very good. Worse than that, only one-third of the suggestions were worth implementing.

"Many companies would have given up at that stage, but Toyota persisted – it should be part of the everyday job, they felt. Twenty years later, they received an astonishing 1,950,000 suggestions in a year, about 32 per person per year on average, more than a fifty-fold increase! Better than that, they were able to implement 90% of them."

"Wow, that's fantastic! I'm amazed," said Philip.

"Of course, many of them represent very small improvements," the Prof. continued, "but the point is this: with no extra money, just by encouragement and good systems, the company had succeeded in getting employees to use their brains as well as their hands. Now making suggestions and improvements has become a daily habit for thousands of Toyota employees."

"But you're not against using money as such, are you? You did say earlier that it could have a real motivational effect applied in the right way."

"Oh, there's no doubt about that, Philip, but it has to be in a format which avoids the worst pitfalls, and *encourages the behaviours you most want to see*," said the Professor affirmatively. I would want it to encourage cooperative working and teamwork, to get both employees and managers working towards the same goals, knowing they would be of benefit for both the company and its people.

"Interestingly," the Professor continued, "we have been looking again recently at a study conducted by researchers in Britain comparing the performance of companies who use profit-sharing as part of their rewards system with those who don't, and the findings are fascinating."

So saying, the Professor switched on the projector on his desk to show a table of data. Philip leaned forward to take it all in.

"The researchers studied 400 publicly quoted companies and decided to compare their performance using purely financial measures," the Prof. emphasized. "This they did over a period of eight successive years (the longest study we have seen of this kind), so the results are not just some one-off flash in the pan. Now have a look."

Average over 8 years	Non-profit sharing	Profit sharing	% difference
Return on sales (%)	5.6	8.4	50.0
Return on capital	15.5	20.6	32.9
Earnings per share	12.8	16.3	27.3
Annual sales growth (%)	13.7	15.5	13.1
Annual profit growth (%)	9.7	13.6	40.2
Annual investor returns	18.0	24.8	37.8

"The profit-sharing companies are better on every single measure, sometimes as much as 50% better, if you look at return on sales, for example.

"Many companies seem afraid to introduce a company-wide profit-sharing scheme – certainly at the time of this study in Britain, a government survey indicated that 79% of companies did not have such a program. But the evidence is stark – the prospect of a profit-sharing money reward can get a whole company working together towards the same goals, and deliver a financial performance which virtually blows the non-profit-sharing competition out of the water."

"Well, these are pretty convincing numbers," said Philip. "I always thought sharing profit would reduce a company's profits, but what this says is companies do much better financially with profit-sharing in place."

"That's right," the Professor confirmed, "these companies are *rewarding the behaviour they most want to see* – namely, cooperation with the company on an everyday basis to improve the performance of the whole business. And it does!"

"But it's not just the money," the Professor quickly added

"Not just the money?" Philip queried.

"No," the Professor continued, "there are other factors which are equally important. These companies take the view that their most important asset is their people – it is they who make all the other assets work. And they treat them differently. Whereas materials, machines and systems respond mechanistically to how they are handled, people respond emotionally to how they are treated and often as a group – and that is a very different thing.

"That's why the researchers themselves conclude that it is the attitude, the participative style of management in these companies – wanting employees to act as partners with their company – plus the profit-sharing that results in these companies having such superior results.

"You see, Philip, it's a balance. Money is certainly important, but how you treat people on an everyday basis is even more important than the money. That is where the attitude of the immediate boss – namely you, Philip – has more influence on employees' behaviour than any other factor. And it doesn't cost you anything. That's where non-financial rewards have a big role to play."

"Non-financial rewards? What sort of thing do you mean?" Philip asked.

"We've been talking quite a while now, Philip, so before we get into all that, I suggest we have a bit of a break. Have a stroll, think about what we've been talking about, and then we'll start again."

Philip was glad of the opportunity. As he walked out into the fresh air, the sun was shining, the grass was green, and it was blissfully peaceful. He spotted an empty bench beneath a great chestnut tree and decided to settle there to gather his thoughts.

***

'Well, that's a principle worth remembering...' thought Philip, *The behaviour that gets rewarded gets repeated*. I suppose I was always vaguely aware of that, but that phrase encapsulates the thing so neatly. And it applies in so many places, at home as well as at work.

'I winced when the Prof. brought up that bit about conceding rewards to your children just to get a bit of peace and quiet. And he's quite right – you're actually encouraging the behaviour you <u>don't</u> want to see. And I suppose when you're not conscious of it, you do similar things at work too, like accepting work which is not quite right or late. You might just be trying to be flexible or kind, but in fact you're just ensuring that you're going to get more of the same in the future. I must ask the other managers about that later.

'When people talked about rewards at work in the past, I had always just thought about money and benefits. The Prof. has certainly made me cast my mind much wider than that. The sense of achievement when you hit a target, finding your boss really listen to what you say, the feeling of belonging when you're part of a good team, these are all very rewarding things emotionally, and I guess we tend to forget how important that is.

'I suppose that's why the Prof. was so heavy about not assuming money was the only solution to every behaviour or productivity problem. When you think about what Toyota achieved by setting up a system for employee suggestions and constantly encouraging people to make it part of their everyday job. I mean, getting an average of 32 improvement suggestions a year from everybody, that's fantastic. We think we're a good company, but we don't get even <u>one</u> suggestion a year on average from our people. Think of all that free input we could get. No wonder Toyota is one of the best car companies in the world...

'These numbers that the Prof. showed comparing the performance of companies who profit-share versus those who don't, was a surprise. Mathematically, you would have thought that those companies who share their profits with their employees would have less profit left at the end of the day. But in that study, it was just the opposite – financially they beat the non-profit-sharers by a big margin. I guess every company wants to get their employees working with them to boost their company's performance, but that obviously works.

'Then there's the non-financial rewards the Prof. mentioned – I wonder what that's all about...it looks like I might be having my eyes opened a bit more...' Still mulling over his thoughts, Philip wandered slowly back to the Professor's room.

* * *

"Well, Philip," the Professor greeted, "do you think you have learned something about the Greatest Management Principle so far?"

"I certainly have," Philip responded, "and it applies in so many places. I mean, I think money rewards are important – look at the differences in the performance of companies who share their profits with their employees versus those who don't. But then look at the incredible amount of improvement suggestions Toyota get from all their employees just by encouragement. So money rewards are not the only thing that works."

"Absolutely right," the Professor replied, "that's why I wanted to talk to you specifically about non-financial rewards. You know, when you are dealing with human beings, Philip, you're not just dealing with creatures of logic, you're dealing very much with creatures of emotion, and these emotions are strong drivers of how people act and react. It's important to have good feelings about work. Do you think people perform any differently when they enjoy their work, Philip?"

"Oh yes, I think when people enjoy their work they tend to do it better, they pay more attention, it gives them a sense of satisfaction. Funnily enough, I think it becomes a sort of virtuous circle – you know, the more they enjoy it, the better they do it, the better they do it, the more they enjoy it, and so on."

"That's a wise observation, if I may say so, Philip. And work can occupy a big part of people's lives - they may spend eight hours a day on it, plus time travelling to and from every day, and maybe even more time thinking about it. So, it's a big part of one's life not to be happy in. That means you have a big responsibility in your job as manager, and it would be good to know just what kind of things produce the greatest job satisfaction, don't you think?"

"Absolutely," Philip quickly agreed.

"Well, some years ago Professor Fred Herzberg conducted some very interesting research on just this subject. He and his research team asked employees in a variety of companies the same open-ended questions and just listened to their answers. This was the leading question: 'Think of a time when you felt exceptionally good or exceptionally bad about your present job or any other job you have had, and tell me what happened.' When they analysed their results, this is what they found.

"The factors which resulted in the greatest satisfaction and good feelings at work turned out to be different from those leading to the greatest dissatisfaction. The 'satisfiers' seemed to fall into the following categories :

- Achievement
- Recognition
- Responsibility
- The work itself
- Advancement
- The possibility of growth

"On the other hand, those factors causing the greatest upset and dissatisfaction – the 'dissatisfiers' – were stories about:

- Company policy and administration
- Supervision

- Working conditions
- Relations with others
- Status
- Job security

"For example, one of the early studies carried out by the researchers was with Pittsburgh engineers, and when they laid their data out in chart form, this is how the numbers looked.

Herzberg Satisfiers and Dissatisfiers
Pittsburgh Engineers

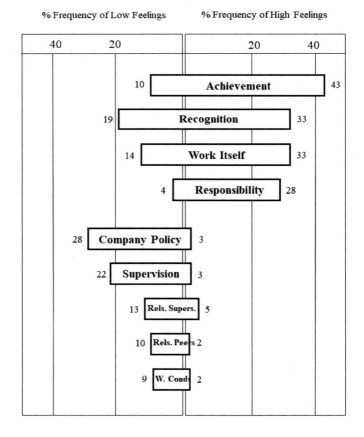

% Frequency of Low Feelings   % Frequency of High Feelings

| 40 | 20 | | 20 | 40 |

10 | **Achievement** | 43

19 | **Recognition** | 33

14 | **Work Itself** | 33

4 | **Responsibility** | 28

28 | **Company Policy** | 3

22 | **Supervision** | 3

13 | **Rels. Supers.** | 5

10 | **Rels. Peers** 2

9 | **W. Conds** 2

"You'll see that the stories about *achievement* weren't exclusively positive, there were some disappointments there too, but by far the great majority were experiences which made the subjects feel 'exceptionally good'. For example, some mentioned team projects they had been involved in at work and the euphoria they felt when they finally cracked problems that had been troubling their company for years.

"Several recalled the first time they were asked to take charge of their department while their boss was away, and mentioned the great sense of *responsibility* they felt as a result. The fact that their boss entrusted them to do the job even temporarily really enhanced their self-esteem, and they remembered it. Similarly, when several respondents mentioned *advancement* – getting promoted to a higher position – they all remembered the actual day and the great feelings it gave them. That's a powerful form of *recognition*.

"Interestingly, many of the scientists and others that the team interviewed noted the attraction of the *work itself*. In other words, they found the work they were involved in so fascinating and challenging that it was a pleasure to come to work. Somehow you feel you are working 'at the frontiers' when you do work like that – it's a challenge that tests your abilities. So when after months or even years of hard work you finally crack a problem like that, it gives a whole lot of satisfaction."

"I can certainly identify with that," Philip responded.

"Now, what does all of this mean for you, Philip? Well, whenever you can, *look for opportunities* to let your people experience just these good feelings. For example, when they achieve some stretching objective which they and you had previously agreed, congratulate them. They may already be feeling good about their success anyway, but your personal praise will just add to these good feelings. That's just one simple example, of course, and you'll find you develop your own way of making these things happen.

"For instance, one manager who came to the college said that he wanted all his people to be 'whistling on their way to work'. By that, he meant looking forward to coming to work because it was interesting, challenging, good at developing their skills, using their ideas, being able to work in a good team and so on. It's great to work for a manager like that.

"Another said he 'treated his people like adults and expected them to behave like adults'. In his case, he told his people he was not going to police them like children, he was going to give them his trust, and expect them to work just as well and as hard when he was not there, as when he was around. And they did.

"But he also told them they could expect him to fulfil his promises and to work hard to get them everything they needed to do a first class job. Creating and earning trust is a big factor in any manager-employee relationship, of course, Philip, so I'm sure that's something you will want to think about."

"No question," said Philip, "what sort of practical things do you think I can do on that front?"

"Well, when we finish this session, Philip, talk to the other managers on that subject, and I'm sure they'll have a bundle of ideas to give you."

"Good, I'll look forward to that," said Philip. "But I'm also anxious to avoid causing all the dissatisfactions that the Pittsburgh folk experienced in their work, so can you give me some more on that subject, Professor?"

"That well-respected management guru, Peter Drucker, once said '90% of what is called management consists of making it difficult for people to get their jobs done.'

"That's a terrible indictment, and Drucker may have been exaggerating somewhat, but I've seen so many examples over the years. You'll have noticed that most of the negative examples in the Herzberg study came under the headings of 'company policy' and 'supervision'. Many times, policies are set by companies to deal with recurrent problems, but their restrictive nature then inadvertently causes even worse problems.

"For example, one aero-engineering company I visited became frustrated at the number of tools disappearing from the production floor, and decided that all engineers in future had to deposit their tools at the end of each shift in the store, and collect them again from there each day. But that led to their losing a half-hour of working time at the end of each shift as engineers lined up to deposit their tools at the store and all the administration and signatures involved verifying who had deposited what. It also meant they lost time in the morning as everyone had to line up at the store to draw out their tools before they could start. Fewer tools disappeared, but productivity plummeted.

"But the biggest problem was the unspoken message the new policy sent. Senior management were effectively saying: 'we can't trust any of you here.' And that is disastrous – in any company! You may not be in senior management yet, Philip, but always remember this: never ever introduce a policy which treats employees as some form of untrustworthy beings, who need herding and controlling. You can take it from me, when trust goes out of the window, so does quality, productivity and customer service. And it's so difficult to get it back."

"Professor, I've got that message, loud and clear. It all seems so obvious when you say it, but trust is quite a hard thing to create...and to keep, I guess. What do you think I can do in my role as manager to do just that?" Philip asked.

"Well, start by assuming that all your people actually prefer to do a good job whenever they can. That's a reward in itself. When people feel genuinely trusted to do a good job, they generally do just that. And that in turn makes them feel good about themselves and the work they do...and the people associated with that work...namely you, Philip. And it saves you a lot of time – you don't have to waste it standing over anybody, supervising.

"You can then get on and do what is your prime job as a manager – namely being a *servant to your people*. That is, working every day to remove all the obstacles and problems standing in their way of doing that good job. And that work is forever – whether it's getting them the training they need, the materials they need, the equipment they need, the information they need, at the time and in the form that they want it, reducing the opportunities for waste, smoothing relations between you and the departments you interface with – the job is endless. And so rewarding, for you and them. It's great working for a manager who does that."

"I can see that, and I'm certainly going to try to do just that," Philip enthused.

"Well, while you're feeling like that, why don't you go and talk to the managers we've lined up for you here. They'll have even more ideas for you."

"I can't wait. I just hope I can remember it all."

"You don't have to remember all the examples, Philip," reminded the Prof, "just the key principle, namely *the behaviour that gets rewarded gets repeated*. And the rewards can be both financial, namely money, benefits, bonuses, etc., but also non-financial – like a sense of achievement, recognition, team success, timely praise and genuine appreciation. And often it's the latter that give the greatest and longest-lasting good feelings about work. And you will have a great deal to do with that, Philip. So, off you go and speak to the managers now."

* * *

'Wow, have I got a lot to learn,' thought Philip, as he emerged from the Prof.'s office. 'I've been vaguely aware of the value of rewards before but never so clearly as how the Prof. put it all. I think I should just try to put a few of these points down on paper before I meet up with the managers.'

So saying, this is what Philip wrote.

- The greatest management principle: the behaviour that gets rewarded gets repeated.
- To be a great people manager, you need to create good associations with work.
- You have to give your people plenty of opportunities to succeed.
- You need to reward/praise/appreciate every notable improvement you see.

- Profit-sharing combined with positive people policies produce superior business performance.
- Avoid like the plague company policies based on staff mistrust.

* * *

Philip's first meeting was scheduled for 2 p.m. with a Bill Evans. As he entered Room 4, he was warmly greeted by Bill with a bright smile and a firm handshake. "So, you've now had your second session with the Prof., have you? Did you learn a few things?"

"I'm learning things all the time here. And I do find the Prof. great at making things clear – that really helps. He keeps saying: remember the principle and the practical actions will follow. So it will be interesting hearing how you folks put that into practice."

"Well, I'm sure the Prof. talked about rewarding the behaviour you most want to see..." Bill tailed off.

"He did," said Philip, smiling.

"I work in the auto industry making parts like radiators, exhaust systems and so on. We like our operators to be multi-skilled – partly because it gives us much more flexibility to cope with absences, sickness and so on, but also because it makes the job so much more interesting for our people. So we have built rewards for multi-skills into our pay systems."

"How do you do that then?" asked Philip.

"To take one section as an example, there are fourteen different jobs there. We divided the skills into three categories – Levels One, Two and Three. Level One means you have mastered five jobs, Level Two ten of the jobs while Level Three means you are qualified on all the jobs in the section. Quite straightforward, but they have to pass the quality test on every job, because we have a 'zero-defects' quality standard at the company."

"<u>Zero-</u>defects?" echoed Philip.

"Yes," Bill continued, "that's the standard demanded these days by our customers. In fact, they have made us well aware that if we ever send them defective parts more than once, we won't be working for them anymore."

"Wow!" said Philip, duly impressed.

"It sure focusses the mind," Bill replied.

"So how long does it take to master all the skills, Bill?"

"About three years, on average. But each new Level earns a permanent increase in pay, so operators are quite eager to take on these new skills. They also get a badge to go with the status, and interestingly, they all wear them. It gives them a sense of achievement, I think, and a real sense of pride. Personally, from observation, I think that feeling is every bit as important as the money.

"We also use an additional bit of money to encourage more of the behaviours we really want to see. It's called a Personal Performance bonus."

"How does that work, Bill?" Philip asked.

"We wanted to make clear what we expected from our people right from the off, the OK Box if you like. So we drew up a list of factors we wanted our people to pay attention to, and to make it worthwhile for them to do just that. This is the actual list." With that, Bill showed Philip the company's Personal Review form.

Personal Performance Review

	Bonus Criteria	Yes	No
1.	Productivity meets standards		
2.	Zero-defect quality level		
3.	Positive response to short-term problems		
4.	Willingness to undertake any job for which he/she is competent		
5.	Helpfulness towards colleagues ('mucking in')		
6.	Makes suggestions / takes initiatives to make improvements in the company.		
7.	Positive attitude to the company		
8.	No absence / Timekeeping problems		
9.	Excellent housekeeping standards		
10.	Personal learning objective achieved from previous review		

"Every six months or so, I sit down quietly with each one of my people and look at how they've done over that time, using this form as a guide. First of all, we pay attention to both productivity and quality – the first because we need to make to a price (the one offered to our customers) and to the quality standard which they demand namely 'zero defects'. Our people are well aware that keeping our customers satisfied is what keeps us in business and protects everybody's jobs, so they all fully understand why that's our focus.

"In production, problems crop up all the time so that's why we have numbers 3 and 5 on the list. We don't want people to wait for their boss to cure all the problems but to act on them immediately wherever they can. Also, if they see a colleague in difficulty, we want them to 'muck in' and help out without being asked. We're all in this together as a team.

"Number 6 is especially important to us. We want everybody to keep an eye out for where we can improve things – where they can make things easier, better or more reliable. I can tell you it makes me much more willing to listen to what they say, in case I miss something useful. And it makes them feel good when they see changes being made as a result of what they have suggested, and even more so when they see it being adopted by everyone in the team. I find the more I listen, the more suggestions I get.

"Another important one for us is number 10. We want everybody here to be learning something more or new every period. We want personal learning and development to become a habit, and this definitely helps to build that idea into the culture of the business. I have to do exactly the same in my job.

"By the way, I don't tell them what they should be learning next. They have to come up with their suggestion of what they want to learn next. Then it's my job to make sure they get the opportunity to undertake the training they want. That way, we find they give their own development serious thought, and they're much more likely to give it the effort required when they're doing it. I should add, it sometimes gives me a headache trying to arrange it all, but I am quite willing to take that job on."

"That's quite impressive, Bill," said Philip, "and do you manage to get everyone living up to these standards?"

"Yes," Bill replied, "although I think the fact that they get a full week's pay as a bonus each time definitely helps!"

"A week's pay?" asked Philip.

"Yes, that comes as a lump sum if they get eighty per cent or more 'yesses' in their review."

"And do they?"

"The record is that between 80-90% of my people get all the money each time. Mind you, it's essential they realise it is not automatic – it has to be earned. If they don't get eight or more 'yesses', they don't get any bonus, it's as simple as that. That's why I do a 'shadow review' each time."

"A shadow review – what's that, Bill?"

"About six weeks before each review, I sit down with each of my guys, and see how they're doing on each of these items. Where they're doing well, I encourage them to keep it up. That's important, I think, when you're doing what can be a rather repetitive job every day. But where they might be falling short, I tell them what they can do to improve, and what they can do to earn that bonus once again. I can tell you that produces quite a lot of positive motivation during the following weeks."

"I'll bet it does," said Philip.

"Our Chief Executive, however, says that although the system is designed to use money and encouragement to reward the behaviour we most want to see, he feels that emphasizing continuous improvement and continuous learning within the system is what builds these habits into the culture of the business. And I really agree with him on that."

"That's a very interesting system, Bill. I can see how that whole thing works very much in your favour," said Philip.

Just then, there was a knock on the door, and a head appeared: "Can I come in, or am I too early?"

"No, come right in James," said Bill, "I'm just finishing here. I'm sure Philip would like a change of speaker."

"No, no, no," Philip protested, "it's been fascinating, it really has."

"Well, if Bill's come to an end now, is it all right if I take over?"

"Yes, go right ahead. Is it all right if I stay, James?"

"Of course, Bill, feel free." James was a rather athletic-looking young man dressed in shorts and sports gear, with reddish hair and carrying a racquet in hand. "I've just been having a game of tennis before I came in, so I've still got my sport kit on, I hope you don't mind."

"Of course not," said Philip, "I'm just pleased you don't mind talking to me here."

"Happy to do it," James replied. "I'm in the food industry, Philip, we make a whole variety of canned products in our company – to be honest I'm often astonished at the millions of cans we send out every day."

"Millions?" Philip echoed.

"Yes, millions," James confirmed, "it's a pretty big plant. Now, I think the Prof. may have told you about profit-sharing companies and how they perform generally."

"Yes, he did," said Philip.

"Well, we're one of these. But I think he also mentioned that they tend to have pretty positive people policies too, is that right?" Philip nodded. "Well, maybe I should start there. Our founder was a bit of an entrepreneur, who was not an academic type of manager by any means – he just had a strong belief in treating everybody fairly and equally. There are differences in pay at different levels in the company, for sure, but everything else tends to be the same.

"For example, there is only one cafeteria (I have to say a good one) – good enough for everyone, even the most important visitors. There are no special car parking spaces – if the Chief Executive arrives late, he just has to walk further to get to his desk. There are no special toilets – one academic visitor called them the best he had ever visited in industry.

"We don't have personal offices. The office is open-plan but with quite a bit of greenery around. The Chief Executive and the Directors sit in a kind of circle in the middle, and then their Divisions spread outwards from there. The old man felt the different disciplines would work better together if they could see each other and communicate easily – that's the basic reason for the format. He also believed that if everybody could see the CEO, they would realise that he was working just as hard as they are.

"Holidays are the same for everyone. Standard is four weeks a year, five weeks after you have been with the company for ten years and six weeks when you have 25 years' service. That means some front-line workers enjoy longer holidays than their Directors. But that's OK as far as we are concerned, they've earned it. Oh, and I should add, everybody clocks in every day, even the Directors and the Chief Executive."

"They all clock in every day?" asked Philip, somewhat incredulous.

"Yes. Mind you, they all get 10% more pay every day for doing so."

"10% more pay? Every day?" asked Philip, even more incredulous.

"Yes. It all started a long time ago when the founder was intent on making sure everyone got everything working straight away in the morning, and it's just continued ever since. Mind you, it works. No one's late in the morning, they all rush to punch that clock, even the Directors. If you pick up the phone at 8.30 to speak to someone, no one's missing, everyone's there. If a meeting is due to start at 2 o'clock, that's when it starts, 2 o'clock."

"Wow," said Philip, "we could do with some of that in our company, I can tell you."

"Anyway," James continued, "that's the background, Philip."

Just then, the door opened. "We're due to meet a Philip Walker here this afternoon," said one, "is he here?"

"That's me," said Philip.

"I'm Janice," said the visitor, introducing herself "and I've brought Marcus here, who's also due to see you too, I think. Sorry to break in, James. Is it all right if we sit in?"

"Certainly," said James, "make yourselves at home. I've just been telling Philip here how we're set up in our company. Now I was intending to take him through our company's profit-sharing scheme. We actually call it our Share of Prosperity Bonus.

"It was introduced a few years ago, and we particularly wanted to keep everything as simple and understandable as possible. We use some pretty tight financial measures in the business, and one of the important ones is Return on Capital Employed – in other words, the profitability we achieve on all the assets and capital we use to run the company. That and total sales are the two measures we use in our scheme.

"We publish a graph very prominently round the company so that in every period (that's every four weeks), everybody can see just how we are doing against our plan. This is how the graph looks...." As he spoke, James projected a slide on the meeting room's wall.

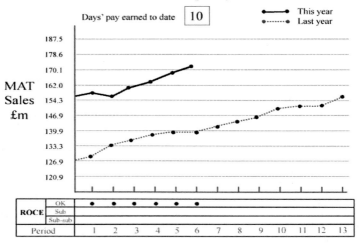

Share of Prosperity Bonus

"Down the left-hand side, the word MAT stands for 'Moving Annual Total' and each of the sales figures represents 5% compound growth each time. At the time of this graph, our sales were increasing at around 20% a year, so we based our bonus 'triggers', as we call them, on achieving four triggers of 5% growth in a year. As you can see, we had achieved two by mid-year. That meant a bonus of five days' pay for everyone each time (so ten days earned so far in this case – that's the figure up top).

"The bonus is expressed as 'days' pay' for basically two reasons. We wanted people to be able to work out exactly what this would mean to them in real cash since they're all familiar with their own pay rate. Also, we wanted them to know that the rate of bonus is the same for everybody i.e.

days of pay – no hidden agenda or special deals for more senior management. We pay out our bonuses twice a year, the first mid-year before the summer holidays and the second just before Christmas. "

"That's a good idea – just when you need it, eh? James, can you explain how the ROCE table below works?" Philip asked.

"That's the profitability measure. Anything 18% or above for Return on Capital Employed would be regarded as 'OK'," said James, "and get the full five days' bonus. Between 14-18 % would only get half bonus while below 14% would get no bonus at all. Needless to say, staff and managers alike are all eager to make sure it stays at a healthy level."

"I'll bet they are," said Philip, "but I'm interested in why you divide it up into four triggers a year, rather just wait till the year end."

"We think a year is too long to wait. We want people to take an interest in the business throughout the year. That's why we mark performance every period. And people start asking questions about our future plans, about why we're doing this or that, and that's good. But we also find that if we indicate that changes that we might want to make could well affect everyone's SOP, they're very willing to help do whatever it takes to keep the business operating in good form. That's a great help, believe me. We just assume people will want to cooperate, and they do."

"That's a fascinating scheme, James," said Philip, "I guess it's what the Prof. talks about when he says you need to be 'making a strong connection between action and reward.' It's certainly clear there, all right."

"Well, we're in the manufacturing industry, but I get fascinated by the ingenuity people come up with in some of the service industries. With service, everything is done face-to-face by all the front-line staff, and the connection with the paying customer is all day every day. It's not easy keeping everybody on the ball all the time. What would you say, Janice?"

"Well, I'm in what you could call the catering industry – we run a whole host of pubs and cafeterias in our business, and I couldn't agree with you more, James. It's tough being bright, efficient and pleasant every day – unless you enjoy the job. And that's what we try to do," Janice responded.

"I'm sure you've had your sessions with the Prof., Philip, and he will have taken you through many of the fundamentals, I guess." Philip nodded in agreement. "Well, we're always trying to give people a bit of recognition or an opportunity to achieve things, as that seems to be what gives people most satisfaction at work.

"We have to remember that it's only a minority of people who do so well at school that they can go off to higher education, get degrees and end up in higher level jobs. The great majority may do OK at school, but it seemed to be the same folks who kept winning all the prizes. Every test seemed to tell them that they were just 'ordinary'. So, we want to give our front-line people a chance, if we can, of distinguishing themselves at work."

"What do you mean, Janice?" asked Philip, his interest stimulated.

"Well, we had some complaints from a big client of ours that the service in their cafeteria was just not good enough in their opinion, and they intended to move our contract to another supplier. That did get our attention, and we sat down to discuss just what we could do to keep them on board. There were a whole load of things we decided to do, but one of these was further training of our service staff. In the process, we decided to give a badge to those who scored well in their training and who could demonstrate giving willing and helpful service to our client.

"I've never been a great believer in badges and things, but every one of our staff who have reached these new standards wear them with pride, I can tell you. Later on, when we organised further training for our staff, we had to produce a silver badge and even later a gold version. I was astonished we had tapped into a real need there, I think, and our reputation with the client just soared.

"Later, staff decided to hold some 'special' days. They arranged a 'Polish Day' where they not only produced a menu with traditional Polish food, they dressed up in Polish clothes too. The client's staff were both surprised and delighted. That led later to an Italian Day and an Indian Day, all in national costume. That client told us that their annual employee survey showed satisfaction with the cafeteria had risen from 39% to 75% over that time. I've learnt a lot by that whole experience."

"It's making me think too" said Philip.

"Among other things," Janice continued, "I've changed my mind about badges. Let me tell you about an exercise we undertook in our pubs. We were looking for ways to persuade customers to visit their pub regularly, and one of the ideas that came up was being able to recognise our customers and call them by their name when they came in. So we set up a challenge to see how many of our staff could 'greet 100 customers by name, and remember one personal thing about them.' When they could, we would enrol them in our '100 Club'.

"Well, within the first month, we had over 100 who could prove that, and we sent out '100 Club' badges to them all. And they found that customers would often ask them what their badge was for, and that would lead to even closer associations with the customer. Our staff liked it, and our customers liked it too. Later we had to start a 200 Club, then there was even a 500 Club, would you believe. One lady even reached the level of 2000 customers known personally! I thought that was fantastic.

"I've long been persuaded about the importance of rewarding the behaviour you want to see, but I often wondered why a simple thing like a badge would be so valued. I mean they don't cost very much, but that's not the point, it's what it represents. It is a <u>visible signal</u> of achievement, and it really means something to people. They wear them with pride, it makes them feel good about themselves – and I have to say it does my heart good to see it. I think that's the kind of feeling it's worth coming to work for every day."

Janice was slightly embarrassed when her little speech drew a little round of applause from the room.

"Sorry," said Janice, "I didn't mean to go on so much..."

"Don't apologise," said Bill, who had been listening intently, "I think you're dead right, Janice. What do you think, Philip?"

"I couldn't agree more, but I'm really impressed by the many different forms reward and recognition can take. I'm getting my eyes opened here."

"Maybe you should listen to Marcus. He might have a few more ideas for you."

Marcus was a young man in his early thirties, with a shock of brown hair and an engaging smile. He began: "I'm in the retail business, Philip, you could say. We sell all sorts of audio-visual equipment, from hi-fi audio equipment to huge TVs, recorders and home theatres. Whatever is the latest in that department, we've probably got it. It's an interesting business as it's always changing and you have to keep moving to stay up to date.

"I know a lot of companies make a big play about giving great customer service, but our founder has been really passionate about that ever since he opened his first shop. In fact he says: 'The primary measure of a business's success should be customer satisfaction, not profits.' He thinks profits are simply an indicator that you're getting the customer service bit right. And you get that message right from when you join the company.

"We have a waiting list for jobs at most of our shops, and you are only offered a job if you get through our initial interviews and one with one of our Directors face-to-face. New recruits attend a three-day course at our headquarters before they ever get to a shop.

"When you get to a shop, you are allocated a 'shadow', who looks after you personally right from the beginning. You are not even allowed to talk to a customer until you have read our customer service manual from cover to cover and can answer questions on it. Initially, you have to wear a 'trainee' badge, and you only get to take it off when you have clocked up 25 'excellents' for service on the survey forms all customers get after their visit."

"Wow, that's a pretty strong message for everyone," said Philip.

"It is, yes," said Marcus. "We want them to be fully focussed on the customer, but we also want to make it rewarding to do just that, and a bit of fun too where we can. For example, come up with a good improvement suggestion, and you'll earn a quick bonus at the end of the month. Get a particularly complimentary comment or letter from a satisfied customer, and you'll earn an even bigger reward.

"But a really special bit of customer service or a really brilliant idea might earn you a gold spitfire badge. Then we tell people in our advertising to look for the guys with the spitfire badges, because they are stars of customer service. And customers do. It's only a small thing, but our staff love that sort of thing – and they can't wait to be the next person to get one."

"Yeah, I might want one of these myself," said Philip.

"Then once a month or so, the company gives each shop £5 per head to take all the staff down to the local pub for an hour to have a 'brainstorm suggestions' session. That can be a laugh sometimes, but some great suggestions come out of that too. One was that we should invite people into our shops to shelter if it's raining, and give them a free umbrella when they go on their way. And we do. Customers are often amazed at that, but they remember it and the shop that did it. Of course, we have free coffee for customers in the shops anyway, but we also offer free ice lollies when it's hot. We make a lot of friends that way.

"The Chairman has had quite a few fun ideas himself. Every quarter, he picks out the two best suggestions we have had, and the winners can enjoy a weekend in a health farm or a trip on the Orient Express. He also established a Five-Year Club, when all of those who reach that service landmark are invited to have dinner with him at the Savoy in

London or the Ritz, and he presents them with a Five-Year Silver Pin.

'Then every month, the top three sales branches get to borrow one of two Rolls-Royces or a Jaguar convertible for the month. Generally, the staff in each branch get to use the cars for two or three days each, and that certainly gets their friends and neighbours talking when they arrive home in such style."

"Hey, that's cool," said Philip, much impressed.

"But we don't want to rest on our laurels, so we conduct an employee opinion survey every year. So far, we seem to get some pretty good feedback. For example, this last year 87% agreed they worked very much as a team in their store; 93% said they were clear about what was expected of them in the job; 91% agreed they received good customer service training in the company; and as many as 98% agreed that Board Directors really believe in the importance of customer service. So, we were quite pleased about all that."

"These are great numbers, Marcus," said Philip, "I don't know how the numbers would turn out if we asked the same questions in our business."

"Well, we're not perfect at everything, I can tell you that, but one good thing about employee surveys is they help you focus on these areas where staff think you might be falling short, and that's really useful. Mind you, every Director of the company has to spend a week every year working in one of our stores. There's nothing better to show you how your company is really working than to spend time on the front line, where the rubber hits the road. And despite all the difficulties and things that can go wrong, we were delighted to learn last year that our sales per square foot were actually the highest of any retail company in the world! Now we're going to have to keep working hard to keep that kind of record."

"Marcus, that's fantastic!" said Philip. The others all added their congratulations.

"Well, we're pleased obviously, but I think it depends on a lot of things. In our case, we do make the OK Box clear and right from when anybody joins us. Ours is obviously about the importance of friendly service, and the training we give spells out what you can do on the front line in a lot of detail. We follow that up with many checks: customer service forms, mystery shopper visits, Director visits, etc.

"Then we encourage suggestions from all employees and give lots of fun rewards for the good ones we get. Hearing about people's trip to the Ritz with the Chairman or someone's experience being able to take a Rolls-Royce home also gets people tongues wagging, as you can imagine. I can't tell you all the things we do to reward people, but this year in our survey, 94% of our people agreed it was fun working with the company. So we're pleased about that."

"I must talk to you more about that, Marcus," said Janice, "with all our restaurants and pubs, we can certainly use a few of your ideas, I'm sure."

"Happy to do that," said Marcus.

"I'm just astonished at these numbers, Marcus," said Philip. "And I can see why so many of you all keep coming back here – you can learn so much from each other. I think I've learned more in these few days than all the training courses I've ever been to."

"Don't get too overwhelmed with it all, Philip," Marcus suggested. "As the Prof. always says: 'Just remember the principle, you'll come up with your own ideas and examples.' And you do. What you have heard from us is what we do, and you might be able to use some of that..."

"Oh, I will, you can be sure of that," said Philip.

"But when you have truly understood the principle, and all the examples just reinforce that, then you will find it affects how you manage for the rest of your life," Marcus assured him.

"I can see that all right," said Philip. "I think I'll go and get my thoughts together now, if you don't mind. Thanks for all your input, folks," said Philip, addressing the others, "I really appreciate it."

* * *

Philip's head was buzzing as he emerged from the meeting room and into the sunshine of the college grounds. 'I think it might be good to make a few notes for myself,' he thought, 'there's so much to remember.'

As he looked at his initial notes, Philip realised they were somewhat random and out of order, but after a number of crossings-out and rephrasing, he had a list he thought would be really useful to him for the future. This is how it looked.

- All these companies use a whole different variety of rewards to encourage the behaviours they want to see:
  o In Bill's case, extra pay for extra skills; personal bonus to encourage high quality, improvement suggestions and further learning.
  o In James' case, respect for all employees through equal status and company profit-sharing.
  o Janice setting challenges for her pub and cafeteria people and seeing their pride in wearing their achievement badges.
  o Marcus rewarding great customer service with all sorts of fun rewards and doing employee surveys to make sure they manage people well.
- And whatever kind of company they are, whatever they do, one big factor stands out to me: they never stop rewarding the behaviour they want to see. That's a big learning point for me.

Chapter 3

Questions–Only Discipline

After two days at college, Philip felt he had already learnt a lot. 'I think if I went back to work now, I would already be doing a whole series of things differently,' he said to himself as strolled in the college gardens the following morning. 'I've only learned about two principles so far – the importance of being clear about the OK Box, and the behaviour that gets rewarded gets repeated – but it's been the details and the examples that have made it all come alive. They really reinforce the principles, I'm not going to be forgetting them in a hurry.'

"Hello, Philip," said a voice, breaking into Philip's thoughts, "I hope we managed to give you a few tips yesterday." It was James, also on a pre-breakfast walk.

"You certainly did, James. You know, I'm very grateful to all you guys for taking the time to tell me all the things you do in your different companies. It was enlightening, to say the least."

"We're always happy to share, Philip. We learn more from each other than anything else, you know. That's why we keep coming back, there's always something new to learn. But, as the Prof. no doubt told you, you just need to remember the principles. You can use some of the ideas you heard here, of course, but you'll develop your own good ideas too, I guarantee it. Do you have one more session to go with the Prof. today?"

"Yes, at 9.30," Philip replied.

"I think that'll be about Q.O.D," said James.

"Q.O.D? What's that?" queried Philip.

"It stands for Questions-Only Discipline," James explained. "It's what the Prof. calls 'maintaining discipline without ever raising your finger'. It's quite a simple process, I use it myself, and I can tell you it really works. But I'll let the Prof. explain all that. C'mon, let's go have some breakfast."

* * *

Philip arrived at the Professor's office spot on time and gently tapped on the door.

"Come in," said a booming voice from within. "Ah, Philip, how are you? Did you pick up a few good ideas from the managers yesterday?"

"A few? You're joking," said Philip, "there were so many my head was buzzing at the finish. Just when I was saying to myself 'that's a good idea', I'd hear about another one and another one. I'm really sold on the idea of rewarding the behaviour you want to see, but I had no idea how many things you could do to do just that. It was inspiring really."

"Well, I'm glad you think so, and although you can make use of some of the ideas you've heard about, I'm sure you'll come up with even more ideas yourself when you get back to the ranch.

"Now, despite all that, there are times when staff don't quite stay within the OK Box, and you have to apply a little discipline, and that's what this session is about. You know, there's a great tendency among managers to think that discipline is about punishing misbehaviour – after all, that seems to be what has been happening in society for centuries. People in authority have tended to use various forms of punishment as the obvious way to get people to conform.

"For example, even your own parents may have had occasion to chastise you at home for various misdemeanours..." the Prof. suggested.

"Once or twice, I have to admit," said Philip with a wry smile.

"Then at school, teachers use detention, setting extra homework or holding pupils back after hours to penalise misbehaviour. The legal system in most countries uses various degrees of punishment in much the same way. You might have been fined yourself for speeding in your car, for example..."

"Oh, don't remind me," said Philip, wincing, "I've already got points on my licence."

"So, it's no surprise then that managers naturally think the way to get people to conform is to punish misbehaviour when they see it. And there's no doubt that can deter, so I wouldn't argue for discarding it. But it's not the best way."

"Not the best way?" Philip echoed.

"No. Effective discipline is not about punishment – it's about getting people to do the right thing. And that's quite different because it changes your tactics completely.

"Let me tell you a story. A few years ago I was revisiting a company, which we had helped win the Best Factory in Britain title, on the occasion of their end-of-year awards party. We heard about some remarkable achievements, and there were congratulations all round. Finally, we came to the 'Employee of the Year' award. To my great surprise, it was awarded not to an employee, but to a front-line manager. And it wasn't a fix, George was the overwhelming choice of the employees themselves.

"What's brought that about?" I asked him quietly later.

"A few years ago, I wouldn't have won anything like that," he confided. "You see, I grew up in a company where I saw managers going around 'kicking ass'. I thought that's what you had to do. So when I was first promoted, I did exactly the same, I 'kicked ass' just like them. But since I've joined this company I've changed completely, I've realized you're never going to get the best out of your people if that's all you do."

"What do you mean?" I asked.

"Well, when you manage by 'kicking ass', people only do as much as they have to, to keep you off their back. They don't take initiatives to help you, on the contrary they quite like it when they see you getting into trouble. If problems occur, they wait for you to sort it out, they think it's your job. If you're not there, they see it as an opportunity to slack off. If you want to keep productivity up, you've got to be there all the time. Come to think of it, I don't know why I ever thought it was a good way of managing."

"So, what do you do now?" I asked. "First, I don't just rely on fear, threats and punishment to keep people in line. What I do is I treat my people like adults, but I expect them to behave like adults."

"But what does that mean in practice, George?" I continued.

"I expect them to do the job the best way they know how – all day every day, whether I'm there or not. Anyone who wants to indulge in childish behaviour, like stealing extra minutes at every tea break and lunch break, getting ready to leave well before finishing time, always waiting to be told what to do when they can see themselves what needs to be done, had better think about finding a job somewhere else because it's not going to be here. I make an assumption that they all want to do a good job every day, and they know that's what I expect of them.

"On the other hand, they know what they can expect of me. I make it my prime task to get them everything they need to do a good job – the right equipment, the right materials, the right information, the right working environment, the right training – that's my job, and they know it. And I bust a gut to get them everything they need, knowing that they'll do a good job for me in return."

"So, it's not just because you have become Mr Nice Guy that you've won this award, then," I ventured.

"No," George came back, "I think I'm quite demanding actually. Going soft is not the answer, people have to know what's OK and what's not OK, and I think they respond to that. But we talk to each other as adult to adult, not as boss to minions, we talk and act as if we're all playing on the same team. They know they can rely on me and I rely on them. I think maybe the reason they all voted for me is that's not what they normally expect managers to be like, and they like the respect it gives them. Anyway, that's what I'm going to keep doing because it really works."

"I was impressed," said the Prof.

"Me too," Philip added.

"What I didn't tell you and I found out from someone else was that the previous week George had brought in a surprise cake, baked by his wife, to say thank you to his team for hitting a target they had been working at for weeks, and he was particularly proud about. His team realised he had been boasting about his team's achievement at home, and his wife was so impressed she decided to bake him one of her special cakes to take in to the guys. That was personal, and they really appreciated that. You see, it doesn't matter how small a reward happens to be, it just needs to be sincere."

"I see why employees would vote for a guy like that," said Philip.

"But I need to explain to you a bit more about using a form of discipline that focusses not on punishment, but on persuading people to keep doing the right thing. Some years ago, an eminent professor contended that there are basically four levels of discipline. This is how he described them."

So saying, the Prof. moved to his whiteboard and wrote:

Prudential

"This is Level One. It's the situation where we all learn from *direct experience* the things to avoid in life. For example, the child goes near the fire and realises it is not only hot, you can get burnt, and that's painful. Or we pick a rose and get pricked or we find these leaves, called nettles, can give you a nasty sting. So we get wise. We find it is *prudent* to avoid situations which could result in pain, suffering or danger.

"Next is…

Authoritarian

"This is Level Two discipline. This is where the persons *in authority* decide what is OK and what is NOT OK. The main decider in this category is the law of the land – over the years, national laws get laid down and govern what is OK behaviour in most countries. But although most conform, people don't always follow the established laws when it doesn't suit them, so you need 'enforcers' to make sure that they do. That task falls to the police in most countries. Then again, they can't be everywhere at once, so not every misdemeanour will be found out.

"That's one of the problems as a manager of relying on authoritarian discipline alone. You have to supervise and police it all the time. But there are plenty of managers who manage just like that. You see, it's seductive to see people scurrying about as you issue orders and call the shots, you feel you are the 'person in authority'.

"But you're never going to get the best out of any team if that's all you do. They'll leave everything to you, and every day you'll find yourself rushing from pillar to post dealing with every little problem because nobody else wants to take any responsibility, and it's tiring, it's exhausting. You don't feel you are making any progress, it's just an achievement keeping all the balls in the air. What you need to do is get everybody working <u>with</u> you, not just for you.

Now, the next level of discipline is…

Social

"At the social level, the pressure exercised by *other people* is what persuades people to conform. For example, fashion has an overwhelming bearing on the clothes that people wear. No one wants to stand out as old-fashioned or fuddy-duddy. Young people especially only want to wear 'the latest' – that's the way to impress their friends.

"Similarly, if mother is going with father to the company's annual dinner-dance, she could wear a perfectly good dress of her mother's, but there's no way she would be seen dead in that. She would have to wear something very contemporary. That pressure is virtually irresistible.

"Often the pressure is similar at school. How often have parents heard: 'Mum, I can't wear these trainers anymore, they're just not 'cool'. I have to have these other (expensive) ones. Mum, please...' Or 'Dad, I have to have that latest iPhone now – everybody at school's got one...except ME. I look like an idiot now.' Most parents resist at first but under constant nagging, eventually concede for peace and quiet. The social pressure is just too great."

"Tell me about it," added Philip. "I've got kids of my own, so I know!"

"However, there are positive social pressures too. For example, if you belong to a club or society, you feel an obligation to follow the rules, to act like a 'good club member'. Similarly, there's usually an energetic urge to do your best whenever you play for a sports team – nobody wants to let the team down, so you're usually quite prepared to put out extra effort to help them win. And of course, you can use that same 'team spirit' at work too, Philip.

"But the final level of discipline I want to describe to you is...

Self

"This is regarded as the strongest, longest-lasting and most effective discipline of all because it is *within the individual* him- or her-self and stays with them permanently. They decide in their own mind what is acceptable behaviour, whether with family or friends or at work, and they live that through every day.

"Now you can always 'exercise your authority' if someone steps out of line, by doing a bit of shouting and throwing your weight about, and the temptation to do just that can be quite strong. But, as I explained earlier, it's hard work chasing after everything and just sets you at odds with your people. What you need to do is to get your people convinced in their own mind that staying within the OK BOX is always the better place to be."

"How can you do that effectively if somebody *does* step out of line, though?" asked Philip. "Some of the other managers were telling me you say you can maintain discipline *without ever raising your finger*."

"That's right," replied the Prof. "In fact if you start wagging you finger or raising your voice in this process, you can regard it as a failure. You have to stay in adult mode the whole time. It's called Q.O.D – Questions-Only Discipline.

"You don't do any telling or laying down the law. You only ask questions, and the aim is to get your respondent to take on the self-discipline – with your help – of managing themselves effectively. You cannot be with them every hour of the day, but they are – and that's the point. Once they accept the need for change in their mind, you will not need to discipline them anymore. They will be their own best managers, that's the aim."

"I like the sound of that," said Philip.

"Well," the Prof. continued, "this is how it works. There are only four questions involved in the process, and they are easy to remember. However, it is quite important how you set up the process.

"Initially, tell the individual involved that you would like a word with them privately. In doing this, your quiet but deliberate demeanour should convey the message that it is about something serious, so it is important not to be smiling at this point. Take them to a neutral location away from their normal work environment (your own office will do if you have one), and make sure you will be undisturbed by telephone or visitors.

"Throughout this whole procedure, stay in adult mode the whole time. That means speaking calmly and firmly and never raising your voice. Shouting is out. Losing your temper is out. Do not wag your finger and act like a sergeant-major, implying 'I could make your life a misery if you don't do as you're told, mate'. That means you are taking back the responsibility for that person's behaviour, and that's not the idea at all. Just accept that by going through this process, you will get a commitment from the individual that will be far more powerful and lasting and give you a far more pleasant working atmosphere than you would get by shouting and threatening.

"Now, here are the questions.

1   Ask: Do you understand what the required standard is?

"Your respondent has to tell you precisely. Just saying 'yes' is not enough. They have to tell you in their own words, specifically. They might hesitate, but press them into it. You have to hear the words coming out of their own mouth, then there is no doubt that they do understand. Explain calmly why the standard is necessary.

2   Ask: Do you have a problem meeting the standard?

"They clearly do, otherwise you wouldn't be there together. If they prevaricate, don't be put off. Insist on hearing what the problems are. Often they find this embarrassing as their excuses are often woefully weak. But don't spare their embarrassment as their discomfort will be a powerful incentive for them not to want to have such a meeting with you again.

"Show you are listening intently to what they say. Indeed, it often helps to have a pad in front of you and to be seen taking down everything they say (yes, it is serious). Don't start criticising or showing your irritation at this stage, otherwise they will clam up to avoid your further disapproval. Just keep asking questions if you need further clarification.

"When you think you have all the problems listed, then say 'All right, let's take each one of these, and see what we can do about them'. Note we are using the word 'we' now, implying that although the responsibility remains theirs, you are now on their side if they are ready to make the effort to resolve them. The task then is to end up with simple solutions to each of the problems they listed, which you think they will be able to carry through. When you are satisfied about each one of these, then move on to question three.

3   Ask: What can I expect in the future then?

"This is an important question. This is when your respondent articulates aloud their personal commitment to different behaviour, and that is fundamental. Do not say what you want. They must tell you what they are going to do in the future. When you finally endorse what they say, it must sound like that they have now 'made a contract' with you, and you should act like that is what it is.

"If the vibes in the session make you feel that your respondent has made a true mental commitment to change, then you can end your meeting at this point. Only ask question four if you feel there is a danger they might default on their commitment, or they have failed to honour previous undertakings.

4   Ask: What will we do if you don't?

"Do not be fobbed off with throwaway answers. For example, if they say: 'No, it's all right, I'm going to do it,' you should reply to the effect: 'Yes, I'm pleased about that, but I'm still asking the same question: What will we do if you don't? Where do you think that could lead?' The best outcome to that question is that they themselves articulate the undesirable consequences they will bring upon themselves if they don't put things right now.

"At the end, they need to feel that the discomfort of this type of meeting is something they don't want to repeat. On the contrary, conformance seems a much easier option all around. At this point you can allow yourself a smile, indicating that you're pleased that the individual has chosen to work with you and do the positive, sensible thing.

"And it's useful to give the person an encouraging touch on the arm as they leave your office just to indicate they can count on your help to keep things moving in a positive direction. You also want them to feel they have been dealt with fairly and are still very willing to be a productive member of your team."

"Effectively you're getting the individual to take responsibility for their own behaviour just by using a series of key questions rather than laying down the law and getting heavy about things," said Philip.

"That's right," confirmed the Prof., "but you have to watch sometimes when they try to pass the responsibility back to you...inadvertently."

"Inadvertently? How do you mean?" Philip queried.

"I remember one of the managers telling us a story about talking to one his people who was a persistent latecomer. Towards the end of his meeting, his team member said: 'I agree, I really need to change, but could you just give me a good kick up the butt if I'm late again?' The answer to that has to be a very swift 'No!' Otherwise they are just passing the ball of responsibility back to you, and you will never be finished chasing. There's no future in that. You are very willing to help them in any way you can, but the responsibility has to remain very much theirs. They have to take charge of themselves."

"I'm beginning to get a new perspective on the subject of discipline with this, I think," said Philip. "I'd always really seen it as punishing misbehaviour, deterrence if you like. But I can certainly accept that external discipline is unlikely to be as effective as <u>self</u>-discipline, if you can get it. I suppose it's just an extension of 'treating people like adults and expecting them to behave like adults'."

"Exactly!" agreed the Professor. "It's not always easy, of course, but if you persist, Philip, that is just what you'll get. Now, why don't you go and have a chat with the managers who are scheduled to meet you now. I think you'll learn a few more things there."

* * *

'Wow,' thought Philip as he emerged from the Prof.'s office, 'every time I talk to the Prof. I get a whole new outlook on the business of people management. And his principles, as he calls them, all seem so simple in concept, but, my goodness, they have some far-reaching effects. I'd better write down a few notes on the discipline subject before I forget them...' This how Philip summarised.

- In a discipline situation, take your respondent to a quiet place, which will remain undisturbed.
- Don't wag you finger, raise your voice or lose your temper. Stay in adult mode the whole time.
- Ask these questions, one by one, and continue till you get good answers.
  - ➤ **Do you understand the standard required?**
    They must tell you exactly what the standard is.
  - ➤ **Have you a problem meeting that standard?**
    Note every problem, and work out a practical solution for every one – together.
  - ➤ **So what can I expect in the future then?**
    Your respondent must make a clear commitment.
  - ➤ **What will we do if you don't?**
    [Only use this last question if it's really necessary.]

Having closed his notebook, Philip wandered off to take a stroll around the college lake. He sat down on a stone and watched the swans paddling round the shore. There was a light breeze coming off the water. He closed his eyes and enjoyed it.

"Getting in a bit of relaxation then, Philip?" called a voice behind him. He turned to look. It was Marcus, one of the managers he had met with the day before.

"Yes," said Philip, "the Prof. sure makes you think in these sessions. It was on 'discipline' today. Mind you, not quite the same kind of discipline as I've been used to up till now."

"I know what you mean," said Marcus, "it's dead easy to lose your cool at times and give people a piece of your mind. You feel better getting it off your chest, of course, but often you just get people's hackles up, and then they go all offended and find ways of getting back at you. It's a hiding to nothing at times. I'm much more inclined to use the Prof.'s way of doing things these days, and I can tell you it definitely works better.

"But let's not dwell on that, Philip. I'm just off to the cafeteria for a bit of lunch. Want to come along?"

"Sure," said Philip, "Good idea. Let's go." And off they went.

* * *

Philip's next appointment was to meet a certain Warren Bates in Meeting Room 3 at 2.00. As he entered the room, he was greeted by a mature gentleman dressed in trainers and a track suit.

"Hello, I'm Warren Bates – you must be Philip Walker..."Philip nodded. "Hope you don't mind – I've just been having a lunch-time dip in the college pool, and I haven't had time to change."

"Don't worry about that," Philip assured him, "I'm just pleased you could come. I seem to be learning something else with every manager I meet."

"Let's hope we can continue, then," Warren replied. "You know, this idea of the Prof.'s of treating people like adults and getting them to take responsibility for themselves is quite powerful. I found it not only helped me hugely dealing with disciplinary situations, it pretty well changed the whole way I manage, I think."

"The whole way you manage? How did that happen then?" asked Philip.

"Well, I work in the aero industry. Things develop and change with great regularity in that business, different problems crop up all the time, it's a pretty pressured atmosphere, I can assure you. I had gotten used to batting off problems as they occurred, dealing with everybody's worries. 'What shall I do about this, Warren? What shall I do about that, Warren?' I would often have a line outside my office, waiting.

"And, secretly, I was actually quite proud about that. 'See how much I'm needed here,' I thought. It made me feel sort of important, you know. In fact, I remember saying to one visitor: 'This place would fall apart if I weren't here.' And in a sense that was right at that time.

"But when I came to the college here, and we had these long conversations about getting staff to take responsibility for themselves and their own behaviour, I suddenly realised I was doing the very opposite of that. I was taking on responsibility for all their problems – and they were very happy to give it to me. They thought: get Warren to give you the answer; that will save you having to think about it. And if you do what he says and it goes wrong, then it won't be you to blame. It was the safest way to go."

"Gee, I might have done a bit of that myself, Warren," said Philip.

Just then, the door opened: "We're due to meet Philip Walker here soon. Is it all right if we sit in, Warren? We won't say a word."

"Yes, come in, have a seat," said Warren. "I've just been explaining to Philip here how for years I'd been solving every last little problem for my people and thinking how smart it was to be the 'big guru' round the place. But I was running myself ragged with it all, I never stopped. There was no way I could keep it going. There had to be a better way.

"That's when I realised that getting people to take responsibility for their own behaviour didn't just apply in disciplinary situations, it could apply just as well to people's everyday habits at work. So I adopted a new strategy.

"When people came asking: 'What shall I do about this, Warren?' I started saying: 'Well you know the job quite well now, what do you think we should do?' and then waited for an answer. They were thrown by this at first, this wasn't the Warren they were used to. They just hadn't been used to thinking for themselves, so for a start, we would sit and work things out together. But I discovered that most of the guys knew what to do already, they just wanted me to tell them – I guess they felt safer that way.

"Of course, it was flattering to have everybody running after me and treating me as the great oracle. But I realised it was just discouraging them from exercising their own common sense or taking any initiatives to help the job along. So this is how we do it now.

"Every time they come up against a problem and want my advice, they have to come with at least two solutions. Then they have to tell me the one they recommend and why. If it makes sense to me, I tell them to go right ahead. Now, it sounds simple, but I can tell you that one thing has literally changed my life. I no longer have to think through every problem for everyone else, I'm no longer inundated with one problem after another. I'd really been mistaking buzzy activity for being effective – and they're not the same. I'm well aware of that now."

"How did you start off with that idea, Warren?" Philip asked. "I guess your people were a bit surprised when you suddenly didn't give them instant answers anymore."

"It wasn't all that sudden actually. I got them all together at one point and told them that from the next week, that would be the procedure for every problem they came up with. If they didn't have some thought-through solutions to propose, they would simply get turned round, shown the door and told to go and think again. It was a discipline actually – for me, as well as them.

"They were not all that marvellous to start with, as you can imagine, but they got better as we went on. Some good ideas popped up, which was great. I remember on one occasion early on, as I was ushering one of my people out of my office, I thought, 'That's a better solution than I could have come up with myself.' That was a revelation. I realised I was actually developing a small army not only doing the job but thinking about it too. Now, that was an advance, using their brains as well as their hands.

"And it's just like the Prof.'s four steps really," Warren added.

"How do you mean?" queried Philip.

"Well, you're correcting a behaviour you don't want to see, and you're getting your people to adopt a new behaviour willingly and to keep it going. It's just adopting a new discipline."

"I think you're right," said a new voice in the room. "In fact, if you don't mind, Warren, I'd like to steal that tactic of yours. I could certainly use it back at the ranch."

"Go right ahead," said Warren, "I'll be only too pleased if it works as well for you as it has for me."

"Sorry, Philip," said the first voice, "we should have introduced ourselves. I'm Michael, and this is Luke. Sorry we were a bit early. You know, every time we sit in somewhere, we learn something else. "

"You're not the only one," said Philip, "I've already decided to use Warren's idea myself when I get back to work, it sounds like a good one."

"I think we've all decided to do that!" said Luke. They all laughed.

"Philip," Luke continued, "we work as Sales Managers, and I thought I could give you a little on how we use the four steps in a sales context."

"Oh, good!" said Philip. "That'll be interesting."

"Selling can be a pretty relentless business, as you can imagine," Luke began, "what with making repeated calls, checking whether certain modifications can be made for the customer, trying to do better than the constant competition, working out complex pricing, doing special deals, writing up orders, checking with head office, it never stops. So, we're sympathetic to what our people have to put up with...but they do need nudging back into the OK BOX from time to time."

"What sort of thing?" asked Philip.

"Not meeting their targets, not making enough calls, not getting their expenses in on time, coming late to team meetings or not appearing at all..."

"Arguing with the trainer on our latest training course," added Michael, "leaving someone else to guess what's missing on an order, failing to turn up to a customer appointment, having handwriting on forms that Finance

Dept. can't read...there's quite a few. Salespeople can be a law unto themselves sometimes."

"We don't go mad about every little thing, of course," Luke continued, "but sometimes we just have to sit down and have a chat. But when we do that, we take the Prof.'s advice – we go private, we go into adult mode, we speak quietly, but we speak serious. Actually, the Prof.'s advice to stay in adult mode all the time has helped us a lot – there's a lot less shouting these days, a lot less raising of voices. We can make our points but still stay friends.

"Also we don't do as much telling – as Q.O.D. says, we just keep asking the right questions. I have found it's quite important to get the salesperson to tell you exactly what the standard is that's expected right at the beginning. It saves any later misunderstandings, so both parties start from the same base.

"When I ask what problems they have meeting this standard, sometimes it's because they're just a bit idle and are not making enough calls. If that's the case and they're embarrassed about it, I don't spare their embarrassment. As the Prof. says: 'Never minimise the power of guilt to get people to do the right thing.'"

"I think I've heard that before somewhere," said Philip, smiling.

"After that, the reasons for their lack of performance can be many and varied. It might be to do with the leads they've been getting (or lack of them), problems with the sales literature, complaints the customer had with a previous order for which they got a hard time, our new price list not being ready on time and causing confusion with the customer, etc., etc. Believe me, I learn as much out of this process as anybody. And I have to make commitments too.

"I see my job as manager as providing everything the salesperson could possibly need to do a good job. So I try to put right anything they legitimately bring up, that's my job, after all. As a result, the meeting becomes more of a 'if you're happy to do this, then I'll do this' collaboration, rather than a mere scolding session. However, when we have covered all the bases, I still ask the question: 'What can I expect in the future then?' And I have to hear what I want to hear, loud and clear."

"Do you ever use the fourth question, Luke?" Philip asked.

"Oh yes," Luke replied, "if we have been through several repeated sessions and we don't seem to be making much progress, then you may well have to do that. Sometimes the person realises they're giving themselves a very hard life facing up to this job they're not doing very well every day, and suffering unwanted managerial attention on top – that's no fun.

"Other times, the individual is just not proving equal to the task, and you just have to move them on. You're always in this dilemma: if you do nothing, then you are tacitly admitting that your stated sales OK BOX is not the real standard at all, and that's a problem. Expect your standards all to go slipping down the slope then, and that's something as a sales manager you just can't allow to happen."

Just then, Luke's colleague Michael broke in: "You want to do the right thing by your people, Philip, of course, but you have to do the right thing by your company too. It's not always an easy balance to strike.

"But it's interesting, one of our salespeople who left us a few years ago popped in to see me the other day. He's doing really well in his new company, in fact he was telling me he just got promoted! He said getting fired from our company was one of the better things that have happened to him. 'You know, the way you do it in these sessions,' he said, 'you only ask questions. But that last one with you really sobered me up. I knew things weren't going to improve in my life if I didn't do it myself, that was clear. So I did. And I've just come to say 'thanks', it's made a difference to me.' I was taken aback, but obviously, I was delighted."

"I'm sure you were," commented Philip.

"You know, all of us managers have had occasion to do a bit of straight talking to one of our staff about something or other, but this 'getting people to take responsibility for themselves' is key, I think. It goes deeper than just a talking-to."

"Tell him about your son, Michael," said Luke, "that was interesting."

"Well," Michael continued, "just about the time we first learned about Q.O.D. I was a bit worried about my son, Ben. He was coming up for twelve and he really wanted to get into High School in our area. But, given the amount of work he was doing at the time, I couldn't see him passing the entrance exam. So I decided to try Q.O.D. on him – no nagging, no shouting, no threatening. Just talking quietly but talking seriously and asking the four questions.

"So, I asked him:

'Did you really want to get into High School?'"

"Absolutely."

'Did you realise what standard you'd have to achieve to get in?'

"I'll have to pass the entrance exam," he said.

'Did you think you would have any problem with that?'

"Silence at this point, and looking a bit sheepish. So we listed the problems together – not many, mainly not putting in enough work, skipping homework, etc. I said : 'OK, let's see what you could do about these. Got any ideas?' Immediately Ben suggested doing some homework every day when he got home from school (that had always been a bugbear). Also instead of fooling about in class with his friends, he could pay more attention in lessons. Naturally I added my support to that.

"So, what should I expect from here then?" I asked.

"I'll put in two hours of study each day between four and six when I come home from school. That way I can get some work done but then still have time later to play some of my computer games.."

"That sounds good to me," I said. "Want any help from me?"

"Not really," said Ben, "it's really up to me, isn't it?"

"Yes, that's right. I can't sit the exam for you, only you can do that. You're really doing the work as an investment in your own future. What do you think might happen if you don't put the work in?"

"Well, I just won't get in," he said.

"And we wouldn't want that to happen, would we?" I suggested.

"No."

"Well, from that day forward, there was Ben getting down to work every day straight from school. I could drop all of the nagging and carping I had been using before, and it worked better! I realized then that Q.O.D. presses you into a different role. Instead of doing big boss or heavy parent – 'you know I know better, so just you do as you're told' – you become much more of a helper and a supporter. And that makes for better relations too. I'm a believer, I have to say."

"I think I am too," said Philip. "And did Ben get in in the end?"

"Yes, he did. We were all delighted. I don't mind admitting I had a bit of a tear in my eye when we saw him go off to the School on his first day, looking very smart in his new uniform. I was really proud."

"I'm sure you were, Michael, any parent would have been," said Philip. "All these examples bring the whole thing very much to life. I want to thank you guys for that."

"That's one big thing about Highfield College, Philip," said Michael. "The Prof. believes principles are not of much value if you can't put them to practical use. That's why although they tend to be simple, when you hear some of the examples, you realise they can often take a whole different variety of forms."

"Can I make a comment there?" asked Warren who had been listening all along. "Hitherto for most of us, discipline meant scoldings, criticism, punishments of some kind. It might mean 'exercising your authority', raising your voice, wagging your finger, making threats even, all with the intention of _discouraging the behaviour you don't want to see_.

But for me, the fundamental difference with Q.O.D. is that you devote all your efforts to *encouraging the behaviour you do want to see.*

And I think that changes how you act completely. Instead of being on a sort of war footing with your respondent, implying threats if they don't change their ways, by only asking questions, you're forced to listen much more, and wait for their commitment. Then you find yourself mentally much more on their side of the table, helping them get where they want to go. That's crucial, I think."

"I go along with that," said Luke, joining the discussion. "I'd just add a couple more points to that if that's all right. I find a lot of the time I've got to fight the urge to act in boss mode and start dictating what I want them to do. But that would mean it's still my objective and not theirs. That's not going to work, I'm going to be chasing all the time. It's only when they spell out what they're going to do, that responsibility passes across the table. And that's the whole objective of the meeting.

"And one more thing. After your session, when you see your respondent actually displaying the kind of behaviour they promised, you need to make positive comments about it, they need to know that you notice."

"You mean you need to keep stroking and encouraging the behaviour you most want to see?" offered Michael.

"Absolutely!" chorused the others.

"I think I've got that message now, guys!" said Philip, smiling. "Thanks for all your inputs. It's been great, I've really appreciated it."

"No problem," said Michael. "I'm sure you'll do the same for somebody else sometime."

* * *

'The Four Steps of Q.O.D. are quite easy to remember,' Philip thought as he emerged from the meeting room, 'but listening to these guys' stories makes it all so much more human and realistic. You can see how it would fit quite a few different situations and still get you the kind of commitment you're looking for without ever having to get heavy about it. Hope I can do that. Maybe I should add a few more notes before I forget.' This is what Philip noted.

- It's important your respondent does most of the talking – they're the ones who are making the future commitments, not you.
- Avoid falling into 'boss' mode and laying down the law. Just keep asking questions till you get the commitment you want to hear. Stay in calm adult mode the whole time.
- Back at work, when your respondent demonstrates the behaviour they committed to, say something positive about it by way of encouragement. Forget about punishing the behaviour you don't want to see – just keep rewarding the behaviour you <u>do</u> want to see.

Going Home

As Philip was packing up ready to go home, his mind wandered over what he had learned over the past few days. 'I don't think I'm going to be the same person after this – I've learned so much in these past three days. But how would I summarise it all when my Director asks me about it? I think I would say the big principles I have learned are:

- You need to make the **OK BOX** clear right from the beginning. Since most people actually prefer to do a good job, once they know what that 'good job' is, that is just what they will do for you. After that my job is making sure they have everything they could possibly need to do that good job.
- **The behaviour that gets rewarded gets repeated**. That's so obvious to me now. Of course, money is one of the important rewards and motivators, but it's not – and shouldn't be – the only one. There are

endless forms of recognition that can enhance one's people's self-esteem, create a bit of fun, celebrate success and give them these all-important *good associations with work*. I'm going to work on that.

- **Questions–Only Discipline** I'd never heard of this before, but, my goodness, I can see the value of that. Getting people to take responsibility for their own behaviour by asking questions only and never raising your voice or wagging your finger forces you into treating your people like adults and expecting them to behave like adults. We can work as a real team now.'

Philip paid a last visit to the college common room to say thanks and goodbye to his many new-found friends. Later, as he drove away through the college gates, he had a smile on his face.